Praise for
Workplace Wisdom for 9 to Thrive

'This wonderful book is loaded with practical, proven methods and techniques you can use immediately to increase your sales and expertise in any market.'

Brian Tracy, Author of *No Excuses! The Power of Self-Discipline*.

'Wow, this book is a breath of fresh air in the world of business books. It's packed full of ideas without the filler and fluff. Even if you have just two minutes you will learn something and it will make you a better leader. Own it and keep it on your desk. You'll be glad you did.'

Dale Beaumont, Founder and CEO, Business Blueprint.

'Nina's decades of passionate study, experimentation, teaching, collaboration and reflection provides the basis for a clear, concise and practical guide. It is a joy to read.'

Jon Pratlett, Neuroleadership Expert, www.JonPratlett.com.

'This is a great book. It's full of tips that will make you better, faster, more successful. Highly recommended for everyone who wants to live a long, happy, productive life.'

Michelle Bowden CSP, Author of *How to Present: The ultimate guide to presenting your ideas and influencing people*.

'Nina Sunday has captured so much practical advice as well as supporting evidence in this book. With so many easy to implement ideas, this book cannot help but boost each one of your nine lives. It is a great read but a better instruction manual on how to succeed.'

Warwick Merry CSP, Master MC, Success Speaker and Business Mentor.

'Nina Sunday has taken a clever look at creativity, personal development, leadership and much more in this book. I found I couldn't stop reading as the ideas, concepts and theories just flowed. She sure got me thinking and reaching for my notepad to scribble down idea after idea that I'm putting into practice right now.'
Lindsay Adams CSP, CEO, Teamocracy.

'Nina has created an on-desk go-to for anyone who wants to stay grounded, easily achieve more and empower new opportunities through mindset and action. Demonstrating her depth and breadth of experience and wisdom, this is a gem of a book.'
Sally Foley-Lewis, Middle Manager expert, www.sallyfoleylewis.com.

'I love your book, Nina. Jam packed with practical tips and take-away tools I could immediately apply. It is obvious you have thousands and thousands of hours studying human behaviour - thank you for serving up your wisdom in such an easy to read format.'
Ian Stephens, Peak Performance Coach, Speaker, Author of *Shift Culture: Delivering business results with a high performance team culture.*

'A wonderfully practical book filled with wisdom to bring the best out of you. Thank you, Nina, for sharing your insights, ideas and inspiration!'
Keith Abraham CSP, Keynote Speaker and Author of *Focus: 4 fast easy strategies for beating procrastination forever.*

'Nina provides her reader with strategies and case studies on how to manage their time, attention and energy. You will find her practical ideas applicable to your personal and professional lives. Pay attention to what matters so you can create significant moments that matter.'
Neen James CSP, Attention Expert, Speaker, Author of *Attention Pays: How to drive profitability, productivity, and accountability.*

'This book gives you bite-size knowledge to feed and satisfy the seeking of wisdom that lives forever inside of you.'

Dean Collier, Author of *The Nine Human Essences: A practical, trusted and reliable method to guide teams, businesses and relationships.*

'Nina makes lifelong learning easy with her pearls of wisdom on know-how. Easy to read, easy to implement and easily the best book on learning essentials; a must read.'

Rowdy Mclean MBA, FAIM, CSP, Global Leadership Expert and International Keynote Speaker, www.RowdyMclean.com.

'This book is a vital read for everyone in business. It offers an enormous number of ideas for better leadership, communication, self-improvement, teamwork and productivity. Whenever I get stuck I am going to pick this book up for an idea to get going again.'

Jenny Cartwright CSP, Author of *Don't Get Hung Up: How To Sell By Phone.*

'Each chapter is an absorbing read in itself, bursting with easy to implement ideas and action steps. Every manager can draw from the insights in every chapter to activate the potential of their team and accelerate results. I have been wanting this knowledge for so long. Well worth the read.'

Avi Liran CSP, Inspirer, Author, www.DeliveringDelight.com.

'I love books packed with lots of practical advice and tips for improving effectiveness in the workplace. Nina Sunday's book is highly readable with a smorgasbord of insights into how to develop better business skills. This book is incredibly useful for the time-poor professional who wants to learn in easily digestible chunks.'

Dr. Irena Yashin-Shaw, Author of *Intrapreneur: How leaders ignite bureaucracy and catalyse change.*

'In Nina's *Workplace Wisdom For 9 to Thrive*', the 12 key topics and bite-size ideas are distilled wisdom, including practical examples on how to implement for greater success.'

Yvonne Collier CSP, Author of *Laffe to Success: A Practical Guide To Getting Along With Others*.

'The fox knows many things, but the hedgehog knows one big thing. This is a book for foxes.'

Chris Golis, Author of *The Humm Handbook: Lifting your Level of Emotional Intelligence*.

'Nina Sunday has penned what at first may seem cryptic tips on communication, yet are the simple everyday stuff we often overlook in our communication but shouldn't – be it verbal or written. As a student of language and its impact on behaviour, I was taken with the Don't statements in the chapter What Word Should You Avoid When Giving Instructions. Plus there's a nice Action section at the end of most chapters to apply the suggestions Nina makes.'

Bob Selden, Author of *Don't: How using the right words will change your life*.

'Workplace Wisdom is like a 30-year journey with Nina. So many good nuggets within the pages from someone who has been there and done that. Like memoirs from the maven.'

Paula Smith, CSP, Speaker, Author, Expert in Presentation Intelligence®, www.PaulaSmith.com.au.

Workplace Wisdom
For
9 To Thrive

Proven tactics and hacks
to get ahead in today's workplace

Nina Sunday

First published in Australia in 2018 by:
Brainpower Training Pty Ltd, Brisbane, Australia. www.brainpowertraining.com.au

The National Library of Australia
Cataloguing-in-Publication entry:

Sunday, Nina

Workplace Wisdom for 9 to Thrive: Proven tactics and hacks to get ahead in today's workplace
ISBN-13: 978-0-9942353-2-9

1. Personal management. 2. General Management. 1. Title 658.3

Edited by Helena Bond
Internal layout by Elizabeth Beeton
Cover design by Elizabeth Beeton
Cover artwork by Praylin Paulraj Shinijah
Cover Image, 'Abstract Hallway with Many Doors', Stock illustration ID: 27559354, Shutterstock.

This book is dedicated to all my friends and fellow authors at Professional Speakers Australia who inspire me to write.

Other works by
Nina Sunday

Brainpower Smart Study:		
How To Study Effectively	Book	ISBN 978 0 9751941 5 7
Time Management	eBook	ASIN B00DE2X34Q
Speed Reading training	Video	ISBN 978 0 9751941 0 2
Super Memory training	Video	ISBN 978 0 9751941 1 9
Customer Service training	Video	ISBN 978 0 9751941 2 6
Time Management training	Video	ISBN 978 0 9751941 3 3
Business Writing training	Video	ISBN 978 0 9751941 4 0

Nina Sunday, CSP*

BA, Dip Ed, Grad Cert (AustFilmTVRadioSchl)   * Certified Speaking Professional

- Nina Sunday, speaker, facilitator, author on workplace know-how
- 1990, founded Brainpower Training
- pioneered Speed Reading and Memory training Australia-wide
- Won *Innovation in Learning* award from the Australian Institute of Training and Development
- Authored five training videos on workplace know-how
- Member: Mensa Australia
- Past State President and board member Professional Speakers Australia

CONTENTS

INTRODUCTION

Predictions around disruption to the world of work declare there is a new work order. Young people today may have 17 jobs in five different careers. Portfolio careers are on the rise i.e. not one job, one employer, but multiple jobs and employers, perhaps over more than one profession.

In a tech world, it's high social skills that help you stand out and get ahead. The best managers are outstanding communicators who know how to lead a team, collaborate with a diverse range of people and able to influence peers and customers to take action. They know it's not what you say but how you say it that makes the difference. Word choice and how we use language impacts the way we persuade others. In the age of disruption, being adept at human interaction is rewarded with higher wages.

Being average at your job is over. Not being interdisciplinary can harm your career. To thrive in a rapidly changing world, managers and teams need to continuously improve all aspects of their workplace know-how: the art of communication and influence, productivity, sales and service, leading people and creating a conscious and transparent workplace culture.

To future-proof your employability in a VUCA world, (short for volatile, uncertain, complex and ambiguous), constant reinvention is the key to keeping up, evolving and staying relevant. Your job IS change. It's up to you to stay change agile and continuously grow and reboot your brain. I trust this book will help you achieve the getting of workplace wisdom.

How to use this book

For managers

Each chapter is a stand-alone piece of micro-learning. Copy a chapter to distribute to your team and invite them to read before the next team meeting. You'll find a list of trigger questions in the article *How to Brainstorm* within the *Stay Curious* section, such as:

- What can we **start** doing?

- What can we **stop** doing?
- What can we do **more of**?
- What can we do **less of**?
- What can we **improve**?

And when you've captured in writing a wish-list of next actions, then rate each suggestion as an A, B, C or D according to its priority, for example:

A. low effort, high payoff – do first
B. low effort, low payoff – do next
C. high effort, high payoff – just get started with the first action-step
D. high effort, low payoff – don't bother

For individual contributors

Show this book to your manager and volunteer to copy a chapter to send around, with your manager's blessing, to team members with the invitation to read then participate in an ideas discussion at the next team meeting.

You might like to suggest your manager leads that discussion, or if they decline, offer to do so yourself. At the meeting, use the trigger questions and record each suggestion in writing as they come up. Allocate a specific time. After idea generation, go back to quickly rate each suggestion as an A, B, C or D priority.

By you taking the initiative this way, (where there's a positive workplace culture), it will likely identify you as a high-potential team member destined for leadership. (However, if this suggestion is not well-received, ask yourself what can be done to make the culture more conducive to growth and learning; or was it perhaps the manner in which you suggested you take the initiative?)

Always be reading

To grow your workplace wisdom read a non-fiction book (digital or print or listen to an audiobook) at least 10 minutes a day. Read at least one book a month, 12 books a year. See the article Read Your Way to the Top in the

Gather Wisdom section of this book for reasons to read every day. Leaders are readers. Be a reader.

Feel free to stay in touch by visiting the contact page at www.brain powertraining.com.au and sharing your thoughts.

The way we did business five years ago can't be the way we do business in the next five. Constant reinvention is the key.

Nina Sunday

Reinvent

MARGINAL GAINS HELPS YOU WIN THE MARATHON OF BUSINESS

Constant reinvention is the key to staying relevant in a world of accelerating acceleration.

Are you familiar with the annual Tour de France cycle race where the peloton, (the main group of cyclists), snakes through the French countryside and villages?

Until 2012, no British cyclist had ever won the race. This lack lustre history changed with Sir Bradley Wiggins' victory in 2012, followed by British Chris Froome winning four Tours de France, 2013, 2015, 2016, 2017, then with Sky Team member, Geraint Thomas, winning 2018. This means British Team Sky won six of seven Tours in close succession.

What explains this amazing run of British wins? It's not luck.

The secret? It started with their coach, Dave Brailsford, applying to cycling the business principle of Marginal Gains, a philosophy of process improvement; improving every little thing by 1%. Accumulation of small 1% gains leads to a tipping point that adds up to an incredible quantum leap.

Team Sky looked at every little detail around cycling and training and asked, *'How can we do this a better way?'* The British team optimised everything. They paid attention to every little detail, and asked themselves, *'Is there a better way to do this?'*

For example:

- equipment: Bike seat ergonomics were studied; they optimised shape of the seat. Tyre weight was improved.
- nutrition: They asked, 'What do riders consume while riding? How can we improve that?'
- weekly training: 'Can the program be revised?'
- sleep: By asking, *'What pillow induces best sleep?'* they identified the best pillow to take with them to hotels.

- massage is part of post-training recuperation: By asking, *'Which massage gel is more effective?'* they found a 1% improvement there.
- health: It's essential to enjoy good health and hygiene. By researching how to best wash their hands they were able to prevent infection.

Continuous 1% improvements over three years led to Team Sky winning its first Tour De France in 2012. To then win six of the next seven Tours de France is not just a lucky streak. It's the result of a culture of finding and implementing small daily improvements.

What can we learn from the success of the Marginal Gains concept? Small daily improvements are key to long-term significant results.

Action

1. **Ask your customers,** 'If we could improve our service even by 1%, what would you like us to do?'

2. **Don't live with bottlenecks, delays or double-handling.** Trial new ways of doing things.

3. **Question everything you do.** Constantly reinvent the way you do things by asking daily, 'How else can we do this?'

4. **Ask who, what, where, when, how and why . . .**
   - Why that way?
   - Why then?
   - Why there?
   - Why that person?
   - How else could this be achieved?
   - Who else could do it?

5. **Remember the Pareto Principle or 80/20 rule.** Fix the top 20% of problems; overall you'll receive an 80% improvement.

   In 1897, Vilfredo Pareto, an Italian political economist, published[1] his observation that 80% of land was owned by 20% of the population. This is now called the 80/20 Rule or Pareto Principle and this 80/20 pattern has since been applied to most aspects of modern life.

For example, in business 80% of turnover comes from 20% of clients. 20% of efforts produces 80% of results. This means, if you have ten things to do, two of them will be more important and yield more payoff than the other eight combined. 20% of your workload are high payoff, high priority items.

A good tactic is to identify the top 20% of important tasks from your list of possible to-dos and devote 80% of your time completing these.

6. **Lead a Marginal Gains brainstorming session with your team.** Empower people to contribute by offering suggestions, thereby 'owning' process improvement. Analyse workflow, identify bottlenecks, eliminate double-handling and duplicating of tasks. This reduces costs and improves efficiency.

It's not about making one big change that has earth-shattering results. It's about all the small choices we make every day that add up over time.

Waiting to implement big changes might mean the 'same old, same old' continues to happen. But if we get into the habit of constantly improving processes, one little bit at a time, it adds up.

Business is a marathon. Shouldn't we all be looking for marginal gains, lots of little 1% improvements, every day that add up over time?

KAIZEN: HOW TO CREATE A WORKPLACE WITH ENERGY AND VITALITY

In the Japanese language 'Kaizen' means 'continuous improvement' — from 'kai' meaning change or to make better and 'Zen' meaning 'good'.

The philosophy of Kaizen comes out of the Toyota Way, a Quality manufacturing approach that grew Toyota into one of the largest vehicle manufacturers in the world.

The goal of Kaizen is to create a workplace with energy and vitality which respects people, provides them with the will to strive, and by doing so, enhances feelings of self-worth.

What Is The Real Work People Should Be Doing In The Workplace?

According to the Kaizen approach, people are at work not just to supply their labour, but also to use their creativity to improve the way things are done.

Continuous small improvements (Kaizen) add up to major benefits: faster delivery, lower costs and greater customer satisfaction.

Tasks are made simpler and easier, speed and efficiency is increased, processes are re-engineered, a safe work environment is maintained and product quality is constantly improved.

The overarching purpose of Kaizen is to create a vibrant workplace with each individual making a contribution.

How to Apply Kaizen In The Workplace

1. Identify Problems To Solve

Ask everyone to look around their own work area to discover small problems. At the same time, consider one possible way to resolve this problem.

Kaizen is not just about finding a problem; it's being creative to come up with a possible solution.

Submit that problem — with possible solution — to the Kaizen Committee. They will meet to consider the problem and suggested solutions and come up with another perhaps more elegant, solution. That committee has authority to take action.

2. Kaizen Board

Under kaizen, all staff are empowered to locate gaps, inefficiencies, and offer suggestions for improvement.

Better than an anonymous suggestion box that people mostly ignore or an invisible online document on your intranet is to place a physical kaizen board in a central area to allow people to add ideas. If you search on the web for the search term, 'Kaizen board', you'll see plenty of examples; but essentially, it's a notice board with four headings:

Ideas	To Do	Doing	Done

Make the board colourful. People are attracted to add fresh ideas to the board and can stay up to date with what the Kaizen committee is doing. Make it easy for people to make suggestions; then get back to them with a response. Include a 'hall of fame' area to display quick wins as they occur, with 'before' and 'after' photos. Recognise the individual who came up with the idea by adding their photo.

Alternatively have an Ideas Board with four segments:

Low Effort / High Benefit	High Effort / High Benefit	Low Effort / Low Benefit	High Effort / Low Benefit

3. Kaizen Committee

A Kaizen Committee can be made up of five to ten team members drawn from different levels of the organisation who are each passionate about change and improvement.

The committee meets weekly for no more than an hour to discuss ideas for improvement from staff and take action to improve the situation.

You can call this group any name you like e.g. 'Process Improvement Group', 'Reinvention Team'.

4. Kaizen Report

A Kaizen report is short and simple. It summarises before and after.

Before: we had this problem.
We took this action.
Effect: it became a little better.

5. Be A Problem-Solver

Toyota once used on their car-making assembly line the Andon cord, an emergency cable made of thin nylon rope hanging on hooks. The first pull summoned team leaders to see if they could fix the problem without stopping the line. An upbeat tune played at the same time. If it couldn't be fixed on the spot, a second pull on the Andon cord stopped the assembly-line to allow time to correct the problem. A final pull on the cord started the line again. The Andon cord became a symbol of Toyota's focus on quality and was copied by other auto manufacturers. You can read more about the Andon cord in the next chapter. (In 2014 the cord which hung like Christmas tinsel was replaced by yellow push buttons.)

Like the Andon cord on Toyota's assembly line, build a culture of stopping to fix problems instead of continuing to ignore bottlenecks or inefficiencies. Empower people to locate a problem worth fixing.

Everyone can become a problem-solver. The challenge of looking for ways to improve makes work interesting, at the same time benefits the organisation.

Kaizen Their Job

Ask people to kaizen their job by continuously asking themselves, 'How can we do this differently?'

THE NUMMI PROJECT: HOW TO CHANGE A CULTURE

NUMMI (New United Motor Manufacturing Incorporated) was a bold joint venture between General Motors and Toyota to build a quality small car in the United States using American workers.[2]

Success And Failure

It's an amazing success story about how to change culture. Yet it's also a cautionary tale about failure to make new ways of behaving stick until they become strong enough to replace old traditions. It's a story about innovation lost.

Joint Venture

What prompted competitors, Toyota and General Motors, to form a joint venture to build a quality, small car in the United States? In 1984, General Motor's market share at the time was seven times that of Toyota's in the U.S., but interestingly, each company had a problem the other could solve.

General Motor's Problem

New government emission guidelines required General Motors to build smaller cars. In the past, small cars were not profitable for GM, due to their poor quality. But Toyota knew how to build quality, small cars that were also profitable.

Toyota's Problem

US Congress was threatening to restrict importing cars to the United States. A way around that is to build cars in the U.S. using American workers. So both companies needed to partner to build a quality, small car in the U.S.

The Old Fremont Plant

Workers at the Fremont plant had the worst reputation in the US automobile industry.

For two decades the plant had made cars and light trucks, but work atmosphere was combative. Grievances were common leading to frequent strikes, absenteeism was high, drinking and drug-taking on the job was rife.

Not only was Fremont car quality poor, so was attitude. Workers might intentionally position loose bolts so they would rattle and annoy the customer.

General Motors had closed the plant in 1982, sacking thousands of workers.

The Toyota Way

As part of the GM-Toyota NUMMI joint venture, planning began for a re-opened Japanese-style plant at Fremont. A re-structured production method would apply principles of The Toyota Way, including emphasis on teamwork and kaizen (continuous improvement).

The General Motors Way

What was the General Motors Way?

Production, production, production. Get volume out. Worry about quality later. If there's a mistake, fix it later.

Never Stop The Line

If a wrong hood or fender was put on, send the car on; fix it later outside in the yard. Workers saw cars with engines put in backwards, cars without steering wheels or brakes. Some cars wouldn't start and had to be towed off the line. Hundreds of misassembled cars with missing parts littered the yard outside the GM plant. Overtime was spent fixing mistakes before these cars could be shipped out.

Quality vs Quantity

Toyota's philosophy was different. Emphasis was on quality. Never overproduce. Never pass on a defect. The last thing they wanted was defects flowing down the line to be repaired later.

Andon Cord

Toyota used the Andon cord, a thin nylon rope hanging above the assembly line. If there was a problem, a pull on the cord requested help from team leaders to fix the problem. Simultaneously, an upbeat tune played. If it couldn't be fixed then and there, the assembly line was stopped with a second pull, to allow time to correct the problem. To start the line again required a final pull on the cord.

How To Change A Culture

Before NUMMI opened, Toyota flew American workers (the same ex-Fremont, 'militant' employees) to Japan in groups of 30 to learn the Toyota system for making cars. Each group of 30 spent two weeks working in the

Toyota plant alongside someone doing the same job they'd be doing back in Fremont.

What Did Americans Learn To Change?

Firstly, Americans are bigger people. Each time they get in and out of a vehicle they're building, it takes an extra second or two compared to a Japanese worker. This makes the American 10-15% less productive.

Focus was on time and motion; how to shave time taken to perform allotted tasks. And if they found themselves struggling to keep up, someone would come over and ask, 'Would you like some help?' That was a turn-around! No-one in a GM plant would ever offer to help. They'd be yelled at for being too slow.

Secondly, emphasis was on how well people work together to solve problems. They learned a new way to work collaboratively as a team. To celebrate end of two weeks of on-the-job training, they held a sushi party. The U.S. workers wearing Toyota kimonos gave their neckties to the Japanese.

It was a symbolic gesture and a powerful emotional experience. Participants left Japan fully convinced the joint venture would succeed.

NUMMI Opened

After only three months, cars coming off the NUMMI line had near perfect quality ratings. Cars made were more reliable and cheaper to make. Grievances and absenteeism dropped. Employees preferred the new teamwork system.

Why weren't lessons learned at NUMMI transplanted to the rest of General Motors?

Instead of deploying the original 16 managers who started NUMMI to train up other divisions within the organisation, lack of strategic plan or vision meant the lessons of culture change were not spread more widely through the company.

Except . . .

There was another Californian plant at Van Nuys which tried to achieve a similar turn-around using Toyota Way principles.

Van Nuys wasn't closed like Fremont had been, but had been threatened with closure. They shut down the Van Nuys plant for two weeks to train everyone in teamwork. But that program lacked the powerful, emotional Japan experiences. NUMMI people had arrived back convinced of the certainty of success. But Van Nuys workers and executives, even after training, still only half-believed they needed to change!

The Result?

Quality at Van Nuys did not improve. GM shut the plant in 1992, with 2,600 jobs lost. Ultimately, in 2009 General Motors became the largest industrial bankruptcy in US history. Its bailout cost US taxpayers more than $50 billion.

So how to explain GM's failure to stop the slide into huge cash losses? There's no easy answer, but factors include:

- GM executives dismissed the trend towards hybrid cars; instead focused on SUVs and trucks. (Sales plummeted when gas hit four dollars a gallon.)
- high cost of worker health care negotiated by the union
- denial over several decades about GM's ever-increasing loss of market share

Harvard Business School professor, Amy C. Edmondson, writes, 'GM was slow to shift its routines and practices in ways that reflected a changing market. The Managerial mindset that enables efficient execution actually inhibits an organisation's ability to learn and innovate.'[3]

And perhaps the biggest reason — they were too slow to apply the lessons of NUMMI. The NUMMI plant produced 8,000,000 quality vehicles, 6,000 vehicles a week, two shifts a day, until 2009 when GM filed for bankruptcy. Toyota took over running the plant alone until 2010, when it closed.

Conclusion

Organisations need to embrace change and accept the need to reinvent themselves before a slide to losing market share becomes a point of no return.

As Jack Welch, CEO of General Electric said, 'Change before you have to.'

THE TELCO THAT SAVED ITS SKIN BY FOCUSING ON THE CUSTOMER EXPERIENCE

Which Telecommunications Giant Is This?

- In 2007 this company posted a loss of $29.5 billion.
- Their American Customer Service Index (ACSI) score was lowest in the industry — 61 points.
- They were struggling to keep their 53.8 million customers happy.
- In 2008, five million subscribers abandoned the company.

Which Company?

It was U.S.-based telco, Sprint, and back in 2007/08 it was struggling to stay afloat. But within five years Sprint had increased its customer service score by ten points to 71 — the biggest improvement of any company in any industry. This score ranked it number one in customer satisfaction. The CEO who led the service turnaround was Dan Hesse. Hesse did two things:

1. **Find And Fix**

   He listened to customers, to find and fix issues that caused customer frustration. Hesse looked at root causes of dissatisfaction and solved them one by one, leading to increased satisfaction.

2. Focus On Customer Experience

He created a focus on the customer experience. In July 2010, Sprint's Vice-President of Customer Experience announced this goal, 'To improve the end to end customer life cycle experience, so that customers would choose to stay with sprint.'[4]

Why is the customer experience so important these days?

The burning platform is disruption. Disruption is everywhere. Newspapers are losing market share. Amazon is replacing bookstores. Ebay is replacing retail. Uber is disrupting the taxi industry worldwide.

As a case in point, Uber focused on friendly drivers, clean cars, lower prices and an improved customer experience. With the Uber app, a passenger could check on their smartphone how many vehicles were in the area before they reserved one, view a map with a graphic of their car approaching in real time, and after the ride, clients could rate their driver.

Booking a traditional taxi, the customer experience hadn't changed in 50 years. You phoned to book a cab, you waited, and you hoped a car was on its way.

What Is Your Organisation Doing To Improve The Customer Experience?

Innovate now — before a start-up upstart disrupts everything.

Lead from the front

Workplace culture is hiding in plain sight.
Is yours toxic or flourishing?

PEOPLE DON'T QUIT COMPANIES, THEY QUIT MANAGERS

Leadership is more a learned skill than an innate talent, and many managers don't know what they don't know about inspiring and leading people.

When a new hire joins a company, their expectations are high. But a common reason they leave is not the organisation; it's their immediate manager. According to Wilson Learning research on employee engagement, happiness at work flows from the leadership skills of managers.

'If managers fail to create job satisfaction within their teams, people feel unmotivated and negative,' says Michael Leimbach, Vice-President of Research and Development, Wilson Learning Worldwide[1]. Managers have the power to create a team that is totally engaged or they can stifle work fulfillment and drive people to leave their jobs'.

There's an even higher correlation between how managers lead and employee satisfaction. The research listed leadership behaviours making the greatest contribution to employee fulfillment. Recognition, feedback and support were identified. Giving direction and setting goals were also high on the list for creating staff engagement.

There's a connection between business results, leadership behaviours and employee fulfillment which impacts competitiveness and profitability. How managers interact with their team on a day-to-day basis is now recognised as a key driver of business performance.

Managers with high emotional intelligence and effective leadership practices create high level fulfilment in their people and keep good staff. This has a direct impact on the bottom line.

According to a report by Aon Hewitt[2], 4 out of 10 employees worldwide are still not engaged. This report links employee satisfaction with performance. Employee engagement is a leading indicator of company growth. Companies that manage higher employee engagement even during an economic downturn, see dramatic, positive impacts to their revenue growth.

BEWARE THE SIGMOID CURVE: HOW TO LEAD FROM THE FRONT

A team leader needs to lead from the front by regularly scheduling a learning meeting most mornings (or start of shift). By asking individuals to discuss and share what's working for them, you set up a collaborative learning atmosphere.

Win Their Hearts And Minds

Leadership is about winning your people's hearts and minds. And it's done by interacting with them face on, tools-down, in a focused and considered way, not barking orders while walking past.

Why is this important?

Answer: The Sigmoid Curve

Charles Handy described the sigmoid curve as an s-shaped curve that corresponds to every human system[3]. The first phase is experimentation and learning, the second period is doing the job, performing well. But ultimately every curve turns downward. The way to curb the downward spiral is to start a fresh, upward curve before the downward direction has gone too far.

The attitude of a team member resembles the s-curve of a sigmoid curve. When they first come on board they are keen, enthusiastic, wanting to do well. But if left alone to just 'do the job', they peak, and effort starts to turn south. Leading from the front starts a fresh sigmoid curve, keeping people enthused.

Taking sales as an example, let's say the typical life cycle of a salesperson in a role is three years. The first year they are learning how to do the job competently. You, as their manager, have their respect. The second year they do the job, you may feel they don't need as much of your input, so you might leave them alone.

If left alone to just 'do the job', third year's performance and attitude may drop exponentially. They either leave, or if they stay on, become actively disengaged. This poor mindset affects not only their own performance, but also others in the team. A manager can prevent a negative spiral downwards by leading from the front, daily. (In some teams, if the leader abdicates leadership, the sigmoid curve might be over three months instead of three years.)

Shalom in the Home was an American reality television series hosted by Rabbi Shmuley Boteach[4]. Over two successful television seasons he helped families overcome problems with communication, marriage and parenting. After installing CCTV into a home, Shmuley would camp outside in a caravan and view family interactions in real time. Subsequently he would give feedback on how parents were interacting with their children, and how spouses were relating with each other. It was a fascinating journey into emotional intelligence.

On one episode, a mother, with head buried in the fridge, barked orders to her children as they walked past. Shmuley showed her how being pre-occupied with fishing items out of the fridge detracted from the message she was attempting to send. Shmuley taught her to stop, focus, and issue specific instructions in a directed, face-the-front way. Changing her approach led to increased respect and compliance.

Action

When and how do you talk to your team? Are you leading from the front?

WANT CHANGE? GO TO YOUR PEOPLE WITH QUESTIONS

Here's The Scenario.

Your organisation announces at a meeting an impending change and asks, 'Are there any questions?' Then dead silence. On everyone's minds might be, 'Why are we making this change?' But fear of being branded a troublemaker keeps their lips sealed.

Management is often threatened by tough questions such as, 'Why should we change? Is this the only solution?'

Change management is not so much about overcoming resistance. It's more about your team accepting a different approach is necessary and asking them how to initiate the change. You are not asking your people to 'buy-in' to a solution, you are empowering them to use their brainpower to come up with one.

Do Not Go To People With Answers.
Go To Them With Questions.

Why don't managers do more of this?

It takes time. Management can often provide a solution more quickly than it takes to discuss the problem and possible solutions.

Emile Chartier wrote, 'Nothing is more dangerous than a good idea, when it is the only idea we have.'[5]

Always Look For The Second Right Answer

Your first response might be knee-jerk.

By going to your team with the challenge, you access innovation and creativity and possible elegant solutions that emerge from exploring root causes of the problem. As well, your people feel as if they are trusted to come up with an answer; that their opinion has value.

Action

Start with the problem. Tell them your whole thought process. It takes more time, but it works.

WHAT ARE THE
8 GOOD BEHAVIOURS
OF MANAGERS?

During early days of the Google company, managers were scarce. It was a flat structure; most staff were engineers and technical experts. In fact, in 2002 a few hundred engineers reported to only four managers.

But over time — and out of necessity — the number of managers increased. Then in 2009, the People and Culture team at Google noticed a disturbing trend. Exit-interview data cited low satisfaction with their manager as a reason for leaving Google. And because Google has access to so much data online they asked their statisticians to analyse and identify top attributes of a good manager.

Creating A Coaching Culture

Google's now famous Project Oxygen started in 2009 as 'the manager project'. The PiLab (People and Innovation Lab) Team researched questions such as:

- How do managers impact team performance?
- Do managers matter?
- How can we create amazing managers, not just competent ones?

Data-Driven

The Google method is always data-driven. PiLab reviewed exit surveys to find out if low satisfaction with a manager was a reason for leaving the company. And conversely, did satisfaction with one's manager correlate with staff staying?

At the time, Google engineers preferred to decode and debug. Talking to direct reports was considered not part of their job; something that got in the way of getting their 'real' work done.

Google surveys already rated managers' performance, from high (top 25%) to low (lowest 25%).

PiLab's research discovered that Googlers (Google staff) on teams of high-scoring managers were not only happier, with higher job satisfaction and retention, but also achieved higher performance and higher scores on innovation, work-life balance and career development.

How Do Best Managers Behave?

Next phase of research asked questions such as:

- How often do you discuss career development with direct reports?
- How do you develop a vision for your team?

Comments in the annual Google Great Manager Award nominations were analysed, as well as thousands of surveys and performance reviews.

Eight Good Behaviours

A set of eight good behaviours common among high-scoring managers were identified.

1. A good manager is a good coach.
2. Empowers the team and does not micro manage.
3. Expresses interest / concern for team members' success and personal well-being.
4. Is productive and results oriented.
5. Is a good communicator; listens and shares information.
6. Helps with career development.
7. Has a clear vision/strategy for the team.
8. Technical skills to help or advise the team.

Be A Coach

What's significant is not just the list of attributes but order of importance. Top of the list is, *A good manager is a good coach*. Last, attribute number eight, is *Technical skills to help or advise the team*.

To upskill managers in these effective behaviours, the Project Oxygen team taught these behaviours in leadership training programs to their managers, and in coaching and performance review sessions with individuals. They redesigned their annual Upward Feedback Survey (UFS) to focus specifically on the eight attributes of great managers.

To gain 'buy-in' from managers across the company, the Project Oxygen team shared the findings and the Action Plan with company-wide presentations to all levels of the organisation — to junior and mid-level managers as well as to Senior Executives. To help managers improve, they described not only the list of attributes but also best practices.

By November 2012, a comprehensive leadership development program of communication and training was in place, cultivating these key management behaviours. Subsequently Google experienced statistically significant improvements in managerial effectiveness and performance.

Upward Feedback Survey

The first Upward Feedback Survey (UFS) listed behaviour statements:

- My manager regularly gives me positive feedback.
- My manager is quick to grant credit to team members for their work.
- My manager does not micro-manage.
- My manager had a meaningful discussion with me about my career development in the past six months.
- My manager communicates clear goals for our team.

'Strongly agree' — 'agree' — 'neutral' — 'disagree' — 'strongly disagree' were possible answers.

The UFS was sent out June 2010 to managers only with more than three direct reports. A few weeks later these managers received an online report with scores including percentage of favourable response for each question, plus comments.

This process kick-started Google's passion in management development, including:

- giving and receiving feedback
- building a vision for your team
- managing change
- identifying a team's core strengths, etc.

Eric Clayberg, a Google software engineering manager, commented, 'I had been managing teams for 18 years. I learned more about managing in six months than I had learned in the previous two decades.'[6]

A comparison of UFS scores from 2010 — 2012 indicated median scores rose by 5%, from 83% favourable, to 88%.

A Google People Analytics manager, Welle, commented, 'We've seen the least effective managers improve the most over time.'[6]

A newly arrived Sales Director managing a global team of 150 people and meeting sales targets, found that his first UFS score, when it arrived, was a real shock. He was surprised to discover that at Google his job was not just about hitting targets. It's also about how he communicates with his team and keeps them focused on long-term strategy. With an action plan and targeted training, that Sales Director was able, over time, to raise his UFS score from 46% to 86%.

Teams

Prasad Setty, Google's Director of People Analytics, progressed to studying teams, looking at questions such as:

- Can whole teams become more productive?
- How much diversity is just right?
- What's the right combination of people who worked well together in the past vs adding new people?
- What else drives people to go from good to great?
- Can we identify preferred personality traits?

People Don't Quit Companies, They Quit Managers.

Larry Page, co-founder of Google, said, 'We should be growing the leaders that the world needs.'[6]

Action

We should all seek to find an answer to the question of how to create truly amazing managers.

Engage

WHAT CAN MAKE YOU A MORE ENGAGING LEADER?

Here's a question for team leaders: How often do you evaluate whether your team is engaged or satisfied?

When team members feel connected emotionally or intellectually to their organisation, they feel more motivated to strive. They go the extra mile.

These days intangibles determine the value of an organisation. Smart leaders now equate productivity with team engagement.

Engagement: Who Is Responsible?

Is it up to the individual to find a way to feel engaged, or is it the organisation's role to create leaders who provide a positive environment for people to thrive and flourish?

According to research[1], leaders do influence the level of engagement within an organisation.

Amongst Leaders Of Highly Engaged Teams, What's Common?

A pattern is starting to emerge:

1. At some point in their careers, engaging leaders have experienced formative experiences that stretched and shaped them.
2. They also think about leadership and hold a set of beliefs about leading.

Engaging Leader Model

The Engaging Leader model[2] describes a set of positive behaviours:

- they step up to lead
- they energise their team
- they connect with people in their team
- they empower and develop their people
- they communicate openly and authentically.

They also have these attributes:

- ability to reflect
- self-awareness
- a sense of purpose as a leader
- a feeling of responsibility for the organisation's success and how well individual contributors achieve
- an understanding of the power of relationships.

When we know precisely which leadership qualities make a difference we can then focus on recruiting into leadership roles those individuals who exhibit such qualities and behaviours.

Action

1. Create a process to measure employee and leadership engagement. (What you measure you can improve.)
2. Recruit or promote leaders who display positive qualities that engage staff i.e. positivity, industriousness, achievement-orientation, enthusiasm and collaborative style.
3. Coach and develop your leaders to coach and develop their people.
4. Re-engage disengaged leaders.

PSYCHOLOGICAL SAFETY: NOTHING ELSE MATTERS IF YOU GET THIS WRONG

What's the one quality or behaviour that most contributes to effective teamwork?

In 2012, to answer that question, Google launched its Project Aristotle[3]. By analysing research studies and observing group dynamics and behaviour of 180 of its own teams, the project's aim was to identify the one thing that makes a team successful.

Looking For Patterns

Google is good at finding patterns. Google was now looking for behaviour patterns of successful teams. They examined, in this order:

1. Is a team successful when members spend social time together outside work? No, that wasn't it.
2. Could it be personality traits, for example, mostly outgoing extroverts or introverted shy people, or right combination of both? Does gender balance play a part? No clear pattern of that was emerging.
3. Does having a strong manager leading a team make a difference or should team structure be less hierarchical? No, that wasn't what made the difference.
4. Educational background?
5. Having similar interests outside work? No significant patterns discovered there.
6. Meeting styles? Some team meetings are more tightly controlled where discussion is not allowed to diverge along tangents. Other team meetings are more free flowing, where attendees interrupt each other. Does that make a difference?

Norms

Finally, researchers started looking at **norms** — unwritten ground rules about workplace culture.

They observed meetings where some teams interrupted one another, with individuals tolerating being interrupted. Other teams insisted on taking turns in conversational order.

Eventually researchers uncovered two behaviours all good teams shared.

Conversational Equality

Firstly, in the course of discussion or working on a task everyone spoke roughly the same amount of time. There was equal distribution of conversation. No one person or small group dominated.

When everyone had a chance to talk, the team did well.

Social Sensitivity

Secondly, people in the good teams displayed social sensitivity, that is, the ability to gauge how other people are feeling by their tone of voice, facial expression and non-verbal cues.

This sensitivity can be measured by a *Reading the Mind in the Eyes* test[4], (often included in emotional intelligence training). This test presents photos of sets of eyes with a choice of four mental states e.g. confused, anxious, bored, amused. The goal is to match mental state with what can be read in the eyes.

These two attributes, conversational equality and social sensitivity, form part of group culture that displays what's called psychological safety.

Psychological Safety

Harvard Business School Professor, Amy Edmondson, first referred to psychological safety in a 1999 study[5]. Edmondson defined it as 'a sense of confidence that the team will not embarrass, reject or punish someone for speaking up.'

How can team leaders ensure psychological safety in the workplace?

5 Ways To Cultivate Psychological Safety

1. Welcome suggestions for improvement and new ideas rather than automatically rejecting them or viewing as personal criticism.
2. Don't tolerate people being rude or discourteous with each other.
3. It's okay for people to share a little about what's going on in their lives. (Don't view it as gossipy chit-chat to be discouraged.)
4. Value EQ (emotional intelligence) as much as IQ (intelligence quotient) and upskill your people in that area with emotional intelligence training.
5. Encourage the ability to communicate and collaborate. (This is now a critical success factor in high-performing teams.)

HOW TO CREATE
A COACHING CULTURE

All managers should ask themselves, 'How can I inspire my team to continually strive to achieve our business goals? How can I maintain momentum?'

The key is getting everyone involved, writes David C. Novak, Chairman and CEO of Yum! Brands, and who, in 2012, Chief Executive magazine awarded Chief Executive of the Year.

Novak describes in his book, 'The Education of an Accidental CEO'[6], how he started regular department meetings where everyone brainstormed how to solve problems and discussed the business.

John P. Kotter, Professor of Leadership, Emeritus, at Harvard Business School and best-selling author on change[7] explains it's important to go to your people with questions, not with answers. If you allow them to co-create a solution they will own the process.

Leadership behaviours that contribute to team engagement include:

- recognition
- feedback
- support.

Setting goals and giving direction are also high on the list.

Strategic

For their companies to succeed, leaders dynamically shape and hone their strategy.

Tactical

Yes, the frontline team should be aware of strategy, but their focus needs to be on tactical execution. Focus their ongoing education in the tactical arena.

For a leader to get more out of their team, one way is to become the coach, personally facilitating growth and productivity. Teaching leaders how to coach can transform their communication style from 'carrot and stick' to adult-to-adult discussion. People excel in such a positive work environment.

Do you want your people to offer out-of-the-box ideas and feel empowered and confident to express what they are really thinking? Then open up channels of communication. Younger workers want to work with leaders they respect; who in return respect them.

5 Ways To Coach Your Team

One to two hours per week spent in short face-to-face meetings (around 10–15 minutes each) with your direct reports is sufficient to lift individual engagement.

You might do one meeting a day or set aside a focused one or two hours per week; whatever works best. In the course of a month, over a dozen team members can be reached

You Can:

- ask about their personal wellbeing and how they feel about success
- share information about business goals or something new coming up
- ask about their career ambitions; get to know their dreams and desires.
- ask open questions and listen.

1. Regular one-on-one meetings with team members are not an interruption; they are an important part of your job. You increase staff satisfaction, and top talent are more likely to stay.
2. Schedule a group morning or afternoon tea; first 10+ minutes for general chit chat and get to know, then call an 'instant meeting' to brainstorm a specific problem.
3. Stand and use a flipchart to record ideas at these instant meetings. You can then display key flipcharts post-meeting.
4. Trigger a group discussion by sending ahead of a team meeting an article or book summary on a business topic — productivity,

communication, customer service or continuous improvement — to pre-read. Start small, but just start and do it regularly.

As David C. Novak would say, 'Get your people aligned. You have to take your people with you.'

TEAM CULTURE HACK: THE MORNING TEA EFFECT

What happens mid-morning in your office?

Do individuals make their own coffee or tea at different times to sip at their desk while continuing working? Group sit-down morning tea disappeared from workplaces in the late 80s and early 90s after it came to be regarded as an inefficient time-waster.

But Brisbane dentist, Dr. Paddi Lund, in his book, *Building the Happiness-Centred Business*[8] describes how morning tea enhances team communication.

Convinced, several years ago I started enjoying team morning tea with my office team, and here's what we discovered:

1. Face-to face communication
   - builds trust
   - increases friendliness
   - reduces tensions
   - creates a positive work environment.
2. It's a problem-solving opportunity. We can gain a group perspective on any issue we are currently grappling.
3. Email clutter is reduced. A quick chat resolves what otherwise might require several to-and-fro emails.
4. After a short break we return to our desks refreshed.
5. Happy staff stay. Increasing enjoyment at work enhances staff retention.
6. Clients enjoy dealing with a business where team members are happy.

Phubbing

But then I noticed a recent trend — phubbing (phone snubbing).

A new staff member at one of his first group morning teas, instead of making eye contact and contributing to the conversation, sat back in his chair looking at his phone while others chatted. I thought about best way to handle this, and here's what I did.

In a private conversation I explained the history of our morning tea tradition; that for many years we quickly grabbed our own beverage and drank it alone while working at our desk. Then I was inspired to institute a group morning tea for enhanced team communication; that we all enjoy the chance to catch up and find out a little about our lives outside of work. At the same time, it can be an opportunity for a mini-meeting for an instant group perspective of an issue.

I also explained that during his lunch break he could check his phone; but morning tea is dedicated to team face-to-face communication. When I explained it that way, he got the message; phubbing stopped.

Morning tea is not a meeting. But held regularly, it fulfils the function of a daily meeting, without calling it so.

If you read articles on how to build a positive workplace culture, you'll read advice such as:

- build trust
- communicate positively and openly
- create team spirit
- be an approachable leader
- give recognition and appreciation
- celebrate personal milestones such as birthdays, birth of a baby or grandchild, or moving into a new house.

All this and more is accomplished with a regular team morning tea.

Action

1. Start group morning tea on Mondays. Then extend it to Mondays, Wednesdays and Fridays.
2. Have a team morning tea in a nearby café weekly or monthly.

3. Occasionally invite people from other departments, either individually or plan a group event.
4. Observe the benefits — increased friendliness, praise and regard, enhanced problem-solving, less friction and blame.
5. And at new staff induction explain the 'team communication' purpose of group morning tea to new staff members.

Influence

PRIMACY AND RECENCY: GIVE INSTRUCTIONS SO PEOPLE REMEMBER

If first impressions are memorable, how can we take advantage of our brain's automatic ability to remember first and last impressions?

In This Article, We:

- play a memory game
- note the results and how it illustrates how our brains remember
- discuss what this means for learning and for life.

Memory Game

To illustrate how your memory works, would you be willing to play a simple memory game? At the end of this article is a list of words. Before turning to the list, first read the instructions that follow.

Instructions

1. There are 29 words in a list at the end of this article. Read each word, one word at a time. Do not memorise. Simply read each word one at a time at a moderate pace. (We are testing natural memory, not your ability to memorise or use a memory strategy.)
2. When finished, and without referring to the list, write down as many words as you can recall. Resist the temptation to look back at the original list.

Memory Game

Now turn to the list of words at the end of this article, follow the instructions, then come back to here to read about the results.

Results

To retrieve five to seven words is a typical result. More than 11 words recalled is much better than average.

Which Words

But rather than focus on how many words you remember, let's ask instead, which words are better remembered? And by observing which words are better remembered, does that tell us how our brains operate?

Primacy Effect[1]

In your written list of recalled words, does *water* or *life* appear? Notice the position of those two words — they start the list.

Most people better remember the beginning of any list. So there's a high probability you accurately brought to mind *water* or *life,* or perhaps the next two words at the start, *ball* and *river.* This is called the Primacy Effect.

Recency Effect

Next, did you recall *rock* or *tree* which end the list? There's a good chance you correctly retrieved the last two words in the list, or the two before that, *dog* and *star.* That's what's called the Recency Effect.

You may retrieve some of the words in the middle of the list, but research shows most people cannot call to mind most of the middle words, except for . . .

Difference

There's a high probability you recalled the word *hippopotamus.* Why? Because it's so different to other words in the list, which makes it stand out. That's another effect of memory, the Von Restorff Effect — anything unusual is better remembered.

Ways To Apply Primacy And Recency

1. Meetings

Start a team meeting with what you want people to recall or action. Do all the scheduling, organising and decision-making in the middle. Then summarise everything to be remembered at end before closing the meeting.

For longer meetings, make sure you schedule a five or ten minute break every 50-55 minutes so people's brains have a chance to refresh before starting a fresh round of information input.

2. Recruitment

Make sure you rate people as you go as your memory may recall only those candidates you met first and last at beginning and end of day or just before or after a lunch break. You may otherwise overlook a seriously good person for the role if they were interviewed in the middle of the day.

Play The Memory Game. Here's The List:

(ACTION: Read it once, then look away and write down words you can remember.)

> water, life, ball, river, apple, sheep, week, rabbit, home, fur, wind, arrow, boat, stone, flower, hippopotamus, cat, door, cow, hat, pen, horse, sun, fish, feather, dog, star, rock, tree.

WHAT WORD SHOULD YOU AVOID WHEN GIVING INSTRUCTIONS?

Whenever we ask anybody to do anything, we are influencing them. We cannot not influence. Nuances of your word choice can have a profound effect on outcomes.

If I say to you, *'Don't think of a blue hippopotamus'*, what's the first thing that pops into your mind . . . ? A blue hippo, correct?

Whatever follows the words 'do not' or 'don't' becomes dominant in your mind.

Neurolinguistics suggests the word 'don't' is ignored by the sub-conscious mind; it's an abstract device of language. What the brain thinks about or remembers are the words immediately following the word 'don't'. Curiously, *Don't forget to return the keys'* is sub-consciously heard as *'Forget to return the keys'*; ('don't' is invisible). If you tell a child, *Don't slam the door'*, it registers as *'Slam the door'*.

Don't Forget vs Remember To

Why is it more common for people to say, *'Don't forget to . . . '* when what they really mean is, *'Remember to . . . '*?

Instead of telling people in an emergency, *'Don't panic!'*, (the idea of panic is now planted in people's brains), the instruction should be, *'Stay calm.'*

Procedures

Knowing this has implications for written procedures.

A sign in a warehouse reads, *'Do not double-stack thin-grade cardboard boxes or they'll collapse.'* But if double-stacking is what they DON'T want them to do, what DO they want them to do? The positive version of the instruction becomes either, *'Please single-stack all thin-grade cardboard boxes'* or *'Thin-grade cardboard boxes can only be single-stacked'*.

The way we use language impacts the way we influence others and their ability to remember important to-dos.

Action

1. Observe with your clients, colleagues and family whether using *'Remember to . . . '* provides a better outcome than *'Don't forget to . . . '*

2. Avoid negation in statements. Phrase things in the positive, describing what you want someone to do, not what you want them to avoid. 'Don't slam the door' becomes *'Close the door quietly please'*; 'Don't forget to return the keys' becomes *'Please remember to return the keys'*.

3. And don't say *'don't'*.

HOW TO CHANGE PERCEPTION BY FRAMING THINGS DIFFERENTLY

How you frame an instruction or question can prime the brain to think a certain way. If one is primed to find flaws, that is what you'll find.

If someone considering surgery was told, either:

'After surgery, survival rate is 90%'

   or:

'After surgery, mortality rate in the first month is 10%'

which statement might more influence their decision?

Answer: people are more likely to accept surgery after hearing of a 90% survival rate, rather than a 10% mortality rate.[2]

Why Is This So?

Each sentence 'framed' the choice differently. The second sentence refers to death after surgery, despite the small percentage.

'Away-from' / 'Towards' Motivations

More people avoid loss, (move away from pain) than seek to gain (move towards pleasure).

Action

To positively influence people, consider how you 'frame' your question with your choice of words.

Quiz

Imagine you are selling meat cold-cuts; which food label will attract the most buyers?

'10% fat'
  or
'90% fat-free'?

Because of the different psychological impact, legislators in the USA considered making it mandatory that if a food label reads '90% fat free', it should also read, '10% fat'.

Framing is about how your choice of words sets up sub-conscious associations that may or may influence the outcome.[3]

HOW TO MOTIVATE WITH TOWARDS VS AWAY-FROM LANGUAGE

'Away-from' people are motivated to move away from what they DON'T want. 'Towards' people are motivated to move towards what they DO want. All human behaviour is driven by moving towards pleasure or away from pain.

In biology, the process of cells moving towards or away from favourable or unfavourable environments is called 'taxis' *(pronounced tak-sis)*. In psychology, this is known as the pain or pleasure motivation. It is also called the 'direction filter', and is part of a person's personality.

How To Spot

When someone states, '*What I don't want is . . .* ', it indicates an 'away-from' preference. If they say, '*What I want is . . .* ' they are expressing a 'towards' motivation. '*I'll never do that again*' is another 'away-from' indicator.

Both 'towards' and 'away-from' individuals may seek the same goal, they are just motivated differently.

For example, to encourage your child to brush their teeth properly you might use a moving away motivator such as, to avoid a trip to the dentist;

whereas a moving toward motivator is to have healthy, well-maintained teeth.

When Communicating

It's natural for a person who is themselves 'away' motivated to use only 'away-from' language in their communication. But this may not inspire a 'towards' motivated individual, and vice versa.

If you are not aware of this underpinning principle, and are a 'towards' personality, you may in fact de-motivate 'away-from' people when describing 'towards' style goals. Conversely, when communicating with a 'towards person' make sure you give them a positive reason why they should do something, (rather than a reason to avoid doing it.)

It's hard to achieve a goal when your thoughts frame it as moving away from what you want to avoid, rather than towards what you do want to achieve.

Leaders with the power to influence communicate with their team using both 'away-from' and 'towards' language, to capture the attention of both styles of people.

Action

1. Improve your understanding of communicating using 'away-from' and 'towards' motivations by noticing which is being used in a TV commercial, magazine ad or even politicians.

2. Next time you:
   - give feedback
   - give instructions
   - write an email

   remember to express yourself in both 'away-from' and 'towards' terms.

3. State personal goals in positive, 'towards' language; what you want rather than what you don't want.

Here's A Short Quiz.

Of the outdoor billboard slogans listed below, which appeal to an 'away-from' motivation, and which appeal to a 'towards'?

Don't leave home without it.

1. Eat more chicken. (Billboard suggests message written by a cow.)
2. Stop destroying our planet.
3. Be a hero. Contribute.
4. Just don't smoke.

(Answers)
Away-from
Towards
Away-from
Towards
Away-from

HOW TO GIVE FEEDBACK USING A 5-STEP VERBAL TEMPLATE

Have you ever given feedback at work only to find it created friction? Or do you sometimes find yourself holding back what you'd really like to say for fear it won't be well-received?

When you notice unacceptable behaviour it can be tricky finding just the right words to comment on that behaviour without making it too personal or criticising the person. Don't just blurt out the first words that come to mind. Plan the best words to use.

Here's a 5-step verbal template to help you communicate feedback in a positive and assertive manner which is neither aggressive nor too passive. An easy way to remember the steps is **B-F-I-R.**

B — Behaviour

1. Describe the facts of the situation by starting with:
    'When you . . . ' [describe the observable behaviour].

F — Feeling

2. Express how you feel about it with:
    'I feel / I felt . . . ' [express a specific feeling e.g. frustrated, disappointed].

I — Impact

3. Explain its impact:
    'Because what happens is, . . . ' [explain the specific impact e.g. 'we lost time'].

R — Request

4. Then ask for a new behaviour:
    'And what I'd like to see in future is . . . ' [ask for the new behaviour].
5. Finish by asking a question, 'What are your thoughts about this?', or 'Would you be willing to do this?'

By phrasing your communication in this 5-step manner, you will achieve better outcomes. Here's an example of how it could go:

When you . . . [came late to the meeting]
I felt . . . [annoyed]
Because . . . [we spent time repeating information the rest of us had already heard]
And what I'd like to see in future is . . . [you arriving on time in future].
What are your thoughts?

This template is just as effective to give positive feedback. Turn it around by changing step 4 to reinforcing the current desirable behaviour, rather than suggesting a preferred new behaviour.

For example:

When you . . . [did such a thorough job in preparing for the meeting]
I felt . . . [proud of your efforts]
And the effect is . . . [the client quickly agreed to our proposal].
I look forward to seeing . . . [more work like this from you in other situations].

This is a Leadership tactic used universally by mentors and coaches. You might like to use it not only with co-workers, but also with family and friends.

Action

1. Rehearse giving feedback using this verbal template so you are fluent and natural before using it in real situations.
2. Give frequent daily feedback using this template til it's second nature. Consider the benefit of frequent, useful feedback on your business culture. Use this template not only with co-workers but also with your spouse, your children and your friends.
3. Avoid using universal terms such as *'You always'* or *'You never'*. Keep the example to one specific event. Read the next chapter for more details on that.
4. Start Step 2 with *'I felt'* or *'I feel'*, not *'you made me feel'*. This is standard practice in counselling and coaching.
5. Don't assign a motivation behind their behaviour. *'I felt disrespected'* *speaks* your truth and describes your reaction, your feeling. Contrast that with *'You were disrespecting me'* which assigns a motivation to the behaviour that may or may not be true. It opens up an opportunity for them to argue that it was not their intention. But how you felt is authentic feedback.

FEEDBACK HACK: WHAT TWO WORDS SHOULD YOU AVOID WHEN GIVING FEEDBACK?

There's an art to giving feedback and here are tips on both what to say and what not to say.

Never Say Never

When giving feedback never say *'never'*, never say *'always'*. Avoid using absolutes — they're annoying and often inaccurate.

For example, if you say, *'You never arrive on time'* or *'You're always late for meetings,'* you will probably elicit a response along the lines of, *'What about the time when . . . ?'* But that's not the point you're trying to make, is it?

It is extremely rare to have 100% never/always events. Feedback should be accurate and balanced. Using 'always' or 'never' indicates a 'catastrophising' thinking style where events are over-dramatised. It switches your listener off.

Stop using unhelpful catastrophising language and use more calming language instead.

Use First Person Statements

It's common to use second-person statements. First person is using 'I' and second person is using 'you'. For example, in popular song lyrics you'll often hear, *'You make me feel like dancing'*, or *'You make me feel brand new'*.

But when giving feedback, avoid second person statements, and particularly the phrase, *'You make me feel . . .* (annoyed, angry, whatever)'.

How you feel in response to the information you receive is your choice (even though it doesn't always feel like it). Take ownership of how you feel and avoid blaming by saying 'I feel' rather than 'You made me feel'.

10 PHRASES TO MAKE YOUR WRITING MORE PERSUASIVE

Ever composed an email to persuade your reader to take action or agree to something? And did you ever wonder . . . is there a secret language of influence?

Here are suggestions re language that has proven effective to achieve a desired outcome. Instead of a commanding tone, use a tone of possibility. Avoid words like:

- you must
- you should
- you ought to
- you have to
- you need to

They come across as 'bossy'. They force the reader to obey.

Humans respond more positively when given the perception of choice. These phrases work better:

- I suggest . . .
- I recommend . . .
- You might like to . . .
- Please . . .
- This language makes you appear a trusted advisor, (not a police officer.)

Persuasive Sentence Starters

Do these sentence starters create an influencing effect?

- If you do decide to . . .
- Would you be willing to . . .
- Are you open to . . .
- I'm wondering if . . .
- I don't know if . . .
- If you can . . . (describe the action) . . . please, I'd appreciate it.

You might like to test how using these sentence starters result in a better response in your recipients.

Increase productivity

GET MORE OF THE RIGHT THINGS DONE

Your job is to get things done. Focus on achieving the top 20% of tasks which lead to 80% of your results. And here's a way to do it.

Steel magnate, Charles Schwab, President of Bethlehem Steel from 1903, was the first American to earn over a million dollars a year. As the story goes, in 1918, when Schwab met efficiency expert, Ivy Lee, he challenged Lee with, 'What can you teach me about productivity, Ivy, that I don't already know?'[1]

Accepting the dare, Lee handed Schwab a blank piece of paper and instructed him to write down his top six priorities for tomorrow. After Schwab listed his six items, Lee next instructed, 'Now number each item in order of priority.' Schwab numbered his list.

Lee explained, 'When you arrive at your desk, start working on your number one item. Stay with it until it's complete or you've taken it as far as you can go. Only then start on your number two item, until it's complete or you've taken it as far as you can go; then your number three item, and so on.

'Cross off each task as it is accomplished, then move to the next to-do on your list.

'As each new action turns up throughout the day, add it to your list according to its priority, while staying focused on your current task, unless that new item is of higher importance than the one you are currently working on.

'At end of every business day, create a fresh list of your top six to-dos, in order of priority, ready for next day, including anything unfinished or new things you've added during the course of the day.'

Lee continued, 'Teach your managers to do a Top Six list at end of every day, ready for next day. And oh, by the way Charles, don't pay me now for this idea. When you are convinced of the value of this system, send me a cheque for whatever you think this idea is worth'.

Five weeks later Schwab invited Lee to his office. 'You remember, Ivy, that efficiency tip you gave me? That's the single most useful piece of advice I've ever had in business. Here's my thank you.' Schwab handed Lee a cheque for $25,000.

This simple Top Six idea helped Schwab grow Bethlehem Steel into the second largest steel producer in the United States.

Five Quick Questions:

1. Do you use a to-do list?
2. Do you prioritise your top six items?
3. Do you create a fresh Top Six list at end of each day?
4. Do you start each day working on your top priority?
5. Do you complete each priority one at a time?

Try these five steps for a week and be amazed at how many more things you can get done in a day; more of the right things.

Observation Exercise

1. Each day for one week, make a note of your starting time for the number one item on your to-do list; your top priority.
2. With each new task, add it as a new item on your to-do list, but keep working on your top priority.
3. Stay with your number one priority until it is complete, or you have taken it as far as you can.
4. Only shift your focus from your current priority task if the new item is more important than the one you are working on.
5. Note the time you complete your top priority item.
6. Repeat this process for your number two item, then number three item, and so on.

Can you see that you accomplish more by focusing on one task at a time?

A final note: don't multi-task. Consider the Zen proverb: *The hunter who chases two rabbits, catches neither one.*

HOW TO STOP MIND CHURN AFFECTING YOUR SLEEP

Do you ever stay awake at night, your mind going over and over all the little things you have to do? This is called 'mind churn', and there's a ridiculously simple way to cure it.

I was working as conference organiser for an international trade conference, and feeling quite overwhelmed; 400 delegates were flying in from around the world. With the event date looming, I felt as if it was a race against time.

My colleague, Muriel, who was more experienced at organising big events, requested I show her my to-do list. I printed it off, she scanned it, then asked, 'Nina, is that absolutely everything?' 'Well no, Muriel, on this list are the most important things; the rest are up here', pointing to my brain, indicating I was relying on memory.

Her response? 'Nina, I only work with people who write down absolutely every to-do.' I thought about it for a moment then responded with, 'I'm busy getting things done. Isn't it a waste of time compiling such a list?' I argued, 'I know what has to be done. I'm doing it. Shouldn't I be trusted?'

Muriel used the broken record response and repeated, 'Nina, I only work with people who write down absolutely everything.' I became more adamant, 'Muriel, you can trust me. I did the last conference. It will be fine!'

Muriel firmly stood her ground. 'Nina, I only work with people who write down absolutely everything.' We had reached an impasse. If I wanted Muriel to stay working on the project, I had to relent.

So I agreed to privately do a pen and paper exercise, what's called a brain dump. I wrote down absolutely everything, every to-do, on one sheet of paper. Surprisingly, it took only 15 minutes. When done, something interesting happened. I looked at my list and every task was there, in black and white, on one page. Something clicked. By seeing a full list, I felt more in control. It all seemed more do-able than before.

Previously, my perception had been that I was under pressure with an endless number of things to do, in a race against the clock. I now felt all was in the palm of my hand.

By getting the monkey off my back, by getting everything out of my head and onto paper, suddenly I felt more relaxed, more in control, more calm about everything yet to do.

And I have Muriel to thank for that. Because if she hadn't insisted, I never would have discovered the importance of writing down absolutely everything.

Action

1. Write absolutely every task down, not just the critical things.
2. Don't rely on memory to remember to-dos; it takes up headspace better used for planning, improving, setting goals, establishing priorities and thinking strategically and creatively.
3. Have a system to capture all your to-dos. It enables your mind to relax, so you feel more in control and sleep like a baby.

DAYBOOK:
THE SECRET TOOL
OF ORGANISED PEOPLE

Have you ever scribbled a note to yourself on a loose piece of paper about a task or good idea, then misplaced it?

Here's a secret of people who stay organised — they keep a 'Daybook' to use during the course of the work day whether phone conversations, quick meetings and notes. If you use a paper notebook for all your daily jottings at your desk, they are then all in one place for later reference. Now of course, a Daybook doesn't mean you can't also take notes on the run on a digital device. I'm advocating a blended, paper plus digital, approach.

On my desk I keep open an A4, spiral-bound notebook to write every little thing as it happens in the course of a day. It's especially good for notes while on the phone.

At start of each day, I simply enter today's date at the top of a new page, usually in large print and in colour. The Daybook keeps track of conversations with or about clients, suppliers, projects, anything, as they come up.

With a Daybook, my file notes are all in one place and can be archived for future reference. Actions are transferred to my to-do list and appointments to my diary.

I can use as many pages as I need; some days spread to several pages.

Some people experiment using different notebooks for different projects. I found I'd inevitably be at a planning meeting with the wrong notebook. So I abandoned a subject-based system for a chronological approach.

Sometimes, for easy reference, I number the pages. I've been known to write up a basic Table of Contents inside the front cover for pages I may want to refer to again, or use sticky notes to flag important pages.

Why not have fun with your Daybook? Use coloured pens to differentiate each day, or create individualised covers by pasting cut-outs from magazines.

Perhaps go to a stationery store and purchase a quality Daybook with an attractive look and feel. Sally McGhee, in her book 'Take Back Your Life'[2] refers fondly to her round, bright red, leather notebook and red ink pen.

Action

1. Buy a blank, A4 size, spiral-bound paper notebook to keep open on your desk as your Daybook.
2. You might like to differentiate the cover by pasting cut-outs from magazines to remind you of your goals — new car, new home, a trip overseas, positive experiences.

THE ART OF DELEGATING

Two quick questions: If you were promoted or left your organisation today, would day-to-day operations be disrupted? Is another team member trained up and empowered to step into your role and take over should you become unavailable?

Embrace Delegation As Part Of Your Job

It enhances your career, leads to promotion and grows the enterprise. By providing opportunities for learning and growth it improves staff morale.

Learn to hand off some of your projects. It frees up headspace for you to plan, improve, set goals, establish priorities and think strategically and creatively.

Have you ever said, 'If you want it done right, do it yourself' or, 'It's faster if I do it myself'? That way of thinking leads to bottlenecks and burnout. Hoarding tasks means your company or division will be stuck at its present level of growth. Embrace delegation as part of your job. Effective, growth-oriented companies have people who excel in delegating as they grow. Better to have a job 80% done by someone else, than 0% done because you didn't get around to it.

Technical competence doesn't attract promotion; nor does doing it all yourself. Delegating does. It's a skill that saves time. To ignore it is to mismanage.

There's an art to delegating and here are a few tips.

1. *Avoid 'Gofer' Delegation ('Go For This, Go For That')*

Allow people to feel like they're contributors to the big vision, not just cogs in a wheel. Give them responsibility for a complete task, thoroughly explained, from beginning to end. They might surprise you with an elegant solution you never considered before.

2. *Take 30 seconds to check understanding*

Ask your delegate to summarise in their own words what the task is, and how it is to be done. One organisation has signs around their office, 'Take 30 seconds', as a reminder to take time to check understanding.

3. *There's more than one way to do it*

Focus on outcomes and timeframe, then allow the person you delegate to the freedom to decide how to do things. Make sure they know if a process exists or any steps that must be completed along the way (such as keeping certain records, or consulting certain people). They might even streamline the process with a useful shortcut.

4. Show appreciation

Handing over an activity, you could instruct, 'I need you to do this . . . because I'm busy!' Or, you could be more persuasive with, 'I understand you have a lot on your plate. But if you'd be willing to assist me get this done, I'd really appreciate it.'

Action

1.   Steadily increase how much you delegate.
2.   Remind yourself that as you train a colleague, you are training yourself to become better at delegating.

THERE IS MORE THAN ONE WAY TO DO IT — TIMTOWTDI

Do you know what's tricky about communication?

For the same set of instructions there can be more than one way to interpret, and you can end up with different results. It can be hard to know if your instructions are 100% clear and unambiguous, until you get . . . feedback.

Can you think of a time you've given someone instructions and they go off and do something quite different? Is it their fault? As the one communicating, perhaps it's your responsibility to remember to check understanding?

One way to confirm understanding is to take 30 seconds, ask them to summarise in their own words what the task is and how they plan to get it done. One organisation has signs around their office — 'Take 30 seconds' — as a reminder to take time to check the task is fully understood.

What To Consider When Delegating

Perhaps 'there's more than one way to do it'? Allowing people freedom to decide how a job is done is a good thing because they may find a shortcut that transforms the process.

TIMTOWTDI (pronounced *'Tim Toady')* is an acronym from Perl, a computer programming language, for, ***There Is More Than One Way To Do It.*** Rather than micromanage, give people responsibility for the entire task, from go to whoa. They may reinvent and improve how things are done.

ADEQUATE
IS THE NEW PERFECT

Tournament chess uses a special clock with two adjacent clocks, each with a button to stop one clock then start the other. Each clock runs separately, never simultaneously.

But did you know competitive chess was originally played without a clock? In early chess competitions of the 1880s, chess masters spent all day deliberating over the next best move. Because it was so boring, spectators who paid a fee to watch the masters asked for a refund. Nothing happened.

When organisers of chess matches introduced a clock, the objective of the game changed from trying to find the best move, to finding the best move *in the time available.* Have you heard of Parkinson's Law — 'Work expands to fill the time available for its completion'.[3] People usually take all the time allotted (and more) to accomplish any task.

Limit the amount of time to perform certain tasks, then do it with velocity.

One organisation asks their managers for a report every Monday. Instead of calling it the 'weekly report' which might take 50 minutes to write, they call it the 'ten minute' report. The goal — to summarise events of the previous week succinctly on one page, and take no more than ten minutes composing it. Instead of pondering each sentence, they just do a brain dump, do it fast and keep writing until time is up.

Use A Timer

For some activities, allocate a specific time and stick to it. Know when to stop.

- 'I will return all my phone calls in one hour.'
- 'I will spend ten minutes clearing this corner of my desk.'
- 'I will take no more than two minutes for each email reply.'

Striving for perfection takes too long. Ask yourself, is this email, is this report, adequate for my purpose?

3-minute / 10-minute Rule

One rule of thumb regarding incoming phone calls is the 3-minute / 10-minute telephone rule. Most telephone calls can be completed in three minutes — unless you are enjoying the conversation, then it's ok to extend it to ten!

When you receive an incoming call, glance at the time and find courteous ways to limit the call to three minutes. You might say, 'I do want to discuss this with you, however, I only have three minutes right now'.

Eventually you can start to disengage from the call by referring to it in the past tense, 'I'm happy we were able to resolve this'. Past tense places the current phone call into the past, 'It was good we discussed this today.' It makes it easier to wrap up the call.

Time Blocks

One way to increase throughput is to organise tasks into time blocks. And cluster the same type of task to do at the same time. Don't jump around from one email to one phone call to something else.

So, how long should you spend on tasks? Do what's adequate for your purpose. Perfection reduces throughput. Understand it's your overall productivity that counts.

Action

1. Make friends with the clock. Note start and end time of tasks and become aware of the time you spend.
2. Keep a log for a week to analyse your workflow and observe your behaviour patterns.

EMAIL HACK:
HOW TO WRITE QUICK SUBJECT-LINE EMAILS

Did you know you can end a brief note in the subject line of an email with the letters 'EOM' meaning 'end of message'? This signals to your recipient the complete message is contained wholly in the subject line.

Thirty-five per cent of email communications are six words or less. Consider these short messages in the subject line:

- 'Planning meeting now 3pm today instead of 4pm. EOM'
- 'Thank you. EOM'
- 'See you at 1pm. EOM'

Tell your colleagues the meaning of EOM — End of Message. It works for me with great success.However, for EOM to be effective, the subject line message should be no more than around 10 words, so 'EOM' can be easily seen. Never cram too many words into the subject line as they'll go beyond what's visible.

EOM.

HOW TO OVERCOME THIS
LIMITING BELIEF ABOUT
PRODUCTIVITY

Do you ever catch yourself saying, 'I don't have enough time'? The belief there is not enough time limits your productivity.

The most important conversations we have every day are those we have with ourselves, our self-talk.

We have negative and positive voices inside ourselves. If you can transform the thought, 'There's never enough time', into 'I always have enough time', you will find it becomes a self-fulfilling prophecy. This positivity releases stress and anxiety and relaxes your mind.

Limiting Beliefs

Having a system to capture new tasks as they come up is a sure way to minimise the limiting belief, 'I get too many interruptions'.

When I deliver workshops on Time Management, sometimes I hear from certain attendees, 'I'm a Creative. Being organised and writing lists cramps my spontaneity.'

I'm a Creative too; I've learned that writing down absolutely everything, combined with working to priority, frees me to follow my passion; what I'm doing today, writing this chapter.

Another limiting belief, 'I can't keep up with technology'. Hello! We don't have to keep up with everything that's happening in the digital world. That's called Shiny Object Syndrome[4] — trying to do too many new things all at once, perhaps not finishing any.

Find one new digital tool and work with it for 30 days. Watch the tutorial videos, attend a webinar if it's offered, stretch yourself by experimenting with its functions.

After 30 days, assess, ask, 'Is this serving me?' If answer is yes, embrace using this tool to support your being organised. If answer is no, abandon it and move on to trial a fresh shiny object for the next month.

Master one new digital tool at a time, and by the end of a year your professional reputation will shift from technophobe to early adoptor!

Action

1. Focus on your top priorities and what you can do in a day.
2. Feel ok about what you can't get done in a day.
3. Observe the language you use when you speak to others, and when you speak to yourself (self-talk). Replace limiting belief negative statements with positive.

Love your customers

LOVE YOUR CUSTOMERS

Business is based on relationships and relationships are based on qualities such as sincerity, empathy and generosity. The most powerful force in business is love.

Love delivers returns way beyond expectations.

It helps the enterprise to thrive, not just survive. It propels your career forward. It provides a sense of meaning and satisfaction in your work. Helps you do your best work.

Just as people can hear you smiling through the phone, they can feel you coming from the heart. We're all here to help each other and get ahead.

Ever seen the bumper sticker practice random acts of kindness? Why not practice random acts of Customer kindness? Not because you expect something in return, but because it's the right way to behave.

The less you expect in return for acts of professional generosity, the more you will receive. Lennon and McCartney said it better than anyone else, 'In the end, the love you take is equal to the love you make.'[1]

WHAT ARE THE MOST COMMON REASONS CLIENTS LEAVE?

Useful lessons can be learned by analysing the reasons clients stop using any business.

A classic research study by LeBoeuf[2] identified five typical reasons customers leave, and here they are:

1. die or move away
2. develop other friendships
3. price
4. dissatisfaction with the product or service
5. attitude of indifference toward the customer by the owner, manager, or staff member.

Can you guess which of these five reasons was cited more often?

Conduct a guessing exercise with your colleagues by asking each person to assign a percentage out of 100 next to each reason listed. (Total percentage for all five reasons should add up to 100%.)

Price

Is price most important?

Many people assume most people shop on price, but research shows only 9% of customers are price shoppers. Price shoppers are not loyal. They switch from supplier to supplier and won't necessarily stay just because you provide good service.

Dissatisfaction

What about dissatisfaction? Is that the main reason to stop using a firm? Not according to the research. Only 14% leave because they are dissatisfied with the product or service, 5% develop new relationships, 3% move away, 1% die.

That leaves 68%.

Indifference

The main reason clients stop using a business is indifference by the owner, manager or staff members.

What behaviour is perceived as indifferent? Lack of eye contact, lack of friendliness, doing one's job in a neutral, humdrum way — these are perceived as indifference.

Last time I flew with Qantas airline, during the usual announcement, 'Qantas flight 508 to Brisbane is now boarding through Gate 8', they added, 'On behalf of Qantas, we hope you enjoy a pleasant flight.'

That's an extra statement that's positive and friendly. It's something a little extra that comes across as 'they care'.

While responding to someone speaking to you face-to-face, if your eyes stay glued to the computer screen, fingers keep tapping the keyboard, it sends a message they are an interruption. Lack of urgency when a client is anxious about a missing or late item is also interpreted as indifference.

The 'moment of truth'[3] principle in customer service highlights that with every interaction your client is deciding whether to do business with you or to continue to do business with you.

Observe for yourself. Are all customer touch points in your organisation positive and friendly?

Action

1. Notice next time you go through a checkout at the supermarket. Did the operator make eye contact and smile? Are they personable?
2. When you answer the phone do you sound welcoming and ready to assist?
3. If you can't say yes to a customer request, can you be creative and come up with a suggestion along the lines of 'but what I can do is . . . ?'
4. Find reasons to stay in touch with regular clients; demonstrate you value this relationship. Create a SIT (Stay In Touch) list.

Customers Say They Want 4 Things:

1. Friendly, caring service, with courtesy and respect.
2. Flexibility and creativity. Never say 'No', cut red tape, make an exception for them and their individual needs.
3. First contact resolution — customers want first person they speak with to solve their problem.
4. Recovery — it's not the fact that the organisation or an employee has made a mistake, it's how you fix it that can 'wow' a customer.

Apologise, fix the mistake within 72 hours, do something extra, and follow up. A complaint is a gift if you recover quickly and creatively.

CUSTOMER SERVICE HACK:

ANSWER THE PHONE
WITH A SMILE IN YOUR VOICE

In the eyes of your customer, every contact is a moment of truth.

A moment of truth, because with every phone call your caller might be deciding whether to do business with your organisation or continue (to do business with you). Have you ever rung a company, and by the way they answered the phone, you felt as if you were an interruption?

How well are your people managing all the moments of truth occurring in your organisation every single day? Is each customer touch point enhancing your image and reputation, or are your people squandering the relationship?

Customer service best practice dictates that you have a standard procedure for answering the phone — and here it is.

When You Hear Any Telephone Ring

1. On the first ring, stop whatever you are doing. Focus on answering the call.
2. On second ring, put a smile on your face. Smiling changes the shape of your face and resonance of your voice. Customers can literally hear you smiling through the phone.
3. Answer after third ring, and never let it go to four rings.
4. Say your company name or division, then your name; for example, 'Asset Services, this is Jim'.

How Memory Works

Memory is a fragile and curious thing. Saying 'Jim speaking' is not as effective as, 'This is Jim'.

'Speaking' as the last word interferes with remembering the person's name.

If you make your name last thing you say, it makes it easier for your caller to remember it. This is because of the Recency Effect[4] — people better remember the last thing they hear.

Using your first name gives your clients a chance to build a relationship with you and your organisation.

Consistency

As well as friendliness, customers value consistency. If one person adds 'How may I help you?' or 'Good morning' / 'Good afternoon', don't all team members have to add that too? So the person going the extra mile in this instance is actually providing inconsistent service; (unless you make it part of 'how we do things around here').

But I'm not recommending adding extra sentences!

When they ring, clients want to know only two things:

- Have I rung the right place?
- Who am I speaking with?

As long as those two things are covered, additional phrases are unnecessary.

Action

1. First ring — stop whatever you are doing.
2. Second ring — put a smile on your face.
3. Answer after third ring with, < Your company or division >. This is < your name >.

Suggestion — find an image of a smile and display it near your phone as a reminder.

DO WHAT YOU SAY
YOU ARE GOING TO DO

With customers, do you do what you say you are going to do? Do you do it when you say you are going to do it?

How common is it for someone to promise, 'I'll find out and call you straight back . . . ' and they don't? Or, 'I'll have it to you by the end of the week . . . ' and it never arrives?

Do what you say you are going to do. Deliver what you promise.

In business, if you say you will do something, you absolutely, every time, must follow through, and get the job done in the time you said you would do it.

And if it can't be done on time . . . let them know. Keeping your client updated on the progress of a task or project keeps everyone happy.

The first secret to being successful in life is building trust by keeping all your promises.

Your customer trusts you when you're reliable, consistent and dependable. Never promise big things then let them down.

Next chapter we'll explore a service tactic of creating a buffer when promising timeframes, so you not only do what you say you are going to do, you get it done a little faster.

MASTER THE PARADOX OF EXCEEDING CUSTOMER EXPECTATIONS

Customer Service is providing a little more than customers expect; exceeding customer expectations by doing a little extra.

But here's the paradox. What initially exceeds a customer's expectations soon becomes the norm. So we must continuously improve standards of service. Companies have got better at understanding what satisfies consumers, so the bar keeps getting raised. As you raise the bar, customers raise the bar yet again.

How do you create a customer who is satisfied with the service you provide? Go the extra mile. Give your customer some extra personalised attention. Be observant and pay attention to details.

For example:

- An auto service company also cleans the windscreen, blackens the tyres.
- A shoe store brings out from the storeroom three sizes of the preferred style of shoe, next size up and next size down. How often are shoes a size too small or too large?
- A bedding company has the delivery team wear disposable booties over their shoes to protect the floors.

And here's the second paradox: a business can't provide the very best service at the very cheapest price. It takes time and effort to provide superior service. However, not to strive to find lots of little ways to update and refresh the customer experience is a business mistake.

Why not make a fast-tracked service available for extra charge? As a case in point, a website hosting company provided only one level of technical support. A customer with a website that was off-air was told by a non-technical, Customer Service person, 24 hours after first complaining the website is off-air, 'We've escalated it to our Senior Technical Team; they will get back to you in 24–48 hours.' Being off-air affects revenue and reputation. To not have a fast-response level of service available for clients who don't mind paying a little extra loses customers. For this hosting company, clients are transferring to other hosts in droves.

Sometimes a service that is too low-level because it is too low-cost, is a business risk, to both client and service provider.

Action

1. What are some examples when you've gone the extra mile for your customer that didn't cost a ton?
2. What's something you can do in your role that is a little extra and unanticipated that doesn't take a lot of time?
3. What's something the client will value but takes only a little extra effort?

UNDER-PROMISE,
OVER-DELIVER
TIMEFRAMES

I responded to a television promotion by purchasing an item over the phone. In these days of fast service delivery, I expected fulfilment quicker than the 14 days I was told it would take to arrive. Still, I mentally locked in 14 days.

When the item arrived in seven days, I was pleasantly surprised and felt good about the company I'd bought from. By building a buffer around promised time of delivery, the company set themselves up for success.

Imagine if they say delivery is seven days. Because that is the promise, when it arrives in seven days I feel neutral; I purchased and we have a social contract they will deliver. But if for some reason there is a delay with mail and item is delivered on the eighth or later day, I would feel negative about the experience.

Timeframe Promises

In their eagerness to please their customer, does your customer service team declare things will happen within the shortest timeframe, one which does not allow for contingencies? Without a time buffer the risk is that you'll either merely fulfil the social contract, leading to a neutral response, or by over promising, set up your client for disappointment. Every day your customer has to wait beyond the promised timeframe they become progressively more negative.

In a theme park, if a ride is advertised with a 30-minute wait, actual wait might be only 25 minutes, or a 20-minute wait might be 15. Isn't this better than being told there's a 20-minute wait and actually waiting 30?

Consider a furniture retailer who orders product from overseas. It's common practice, when the shipping container becomes full, even before all items are packed, remaining orders are carried over to the next container. Aren't staff better off to say it takes '12 weeks or less' to arrive, rather than give a low-high range such as '8 to 12 weeks to arrive'? Will your client consider it 'late' after 8 weeks, one day?

Same day promises are similar. Instead of verbally committing to sending it 'straight away', say 'soon' instead. Perhaps find out first, 'When do you need this by?' Your client might surprise you with, 'I'm out of office next week, so don't send until . . . '

Alternatively, if the reply is along the lines of, 'I have a meeting tomorrow at 9 am where I'll need the information', then you know this is a priority to get done with urgency.

Another way to apply this tactic . . . your customer wants something done *fast*. You estimate it will take one hour to complete, assuming no interruptions. Let your client know you'll get onto this, but promise completion in two hours.

When you are finished in one hour as you anticipated, your client will be delighted you were so prompt. And if for any reason you are interrupted, you have allowed yourself a buffer, so you can still appear efficient and professional.

Vary timeframes as appropriate; promise 'by end of the week' yet send it to them tomorrow. This gives you extra time should an unanticipated delay arise.

What Not To Do

A holiday resort would surprise repeat guests with an unexpected fruit hamper in their room. This created customer delight and goodwill. But then Marketing decided to promote in the new brochure, 'free fruit basket to repeat guests upon arrival.' That's when lack of appreciation manifested.

- 'It's not very big, is it?'
- 'I don't like bananas; can I swap for oranges?'

The lesson here is to think of something a little extra you can give or do without informing your client ahead of time. It's not part of the package, they didn't pay for it, they don't know about it, therefore it's not expected and more likely to be appreciated.

How Much Appreciation Can We Expect?

In everything there is a balance.

Social psychologists are researching under-promising and over-delivering.[5] Clients are not as grateful as we might expect when promises are exceeded. Going the extra mile is touted as a customer service golden rule; yet what clients want is to have their expectations met. Yes, you want to avoid negative feelings generated by disappointing a customer; but don't expect that same customer to actively express gratitude or appreciation when their request is exceeded. Customers are only human. So exceed expectations, but only just a little.

Action

1. When making any time promise, when appropriate, be non-specific and include a buffer around the timeframe. Use phrases such as 'today or tomorrow' or 'soon'. Then get it done as soon as you can, as if you'd promised your client 'today'.
2. Think of three ways you can under-promise and over-deliver timeframes in your role.

HOW TO SAY 'NO' TO CLIENTS WITHOUT USING THE 'NO' WORD

It's good to be flexible with customers and make exceptions to rules. But how do you say 'no' to someone when you just cannot agree to what they are asking for? How can you manage client expectations? *How* you say 'no' can make all the difference between keeping a customer or losing them.

Here is a 4-step process using the example of a customer wanting you to extend an expired warranty on a camera so it can be repaired at no charge:

Step 1.

Don't say 'no', instead tell them you wish you could do what they are asking for . . . (*'I wish I could . . . '* OR *'I know you would like us to . . . '*)

Step 2.

Use the word 'but' and give a neutral reason.

Step 3:

Use the word 'but' again, and this time tell them what you *can* do for them. ('. . . *but what I* **can** *do is* . . . ').

Step 4:

Diarise what you say you are going to do and deliver whatever you have promised.

Remember To:

- speak with confidence
- apologise . . . and sound sincere.
- have empathy . . . and sound empathetic
- deliver the action you promise.

For example:

1. 'I wish I could extend the warranty on this camera so it can be repaired at no charge' or 'I know you would like us to extend the warranty on this camera so it can be repaired at no charge'
2. '. . . but the manufacturer doesn't allow us to . . .'
3. '. . . but what I **can** do is arrange for a quote from the workshop at no charge, so you only pay if you decide to go ahead with the repair.'
4. Keep track of your promise by adding it to your to-do list.

Most reasonable clients know it isn't always possible for you to say 'yes' every request. If you give them a reason, explaining it in friendly fashion, with empathy, then they are more likely to accept a 'no'.

Communicate

'Look for the clutter in your writing and prune it ruthlessly.'

William Zinsser,
On Writing Well: The Classic Guide to Writing Nonfiction

THE TOP 5 COMPLAINTS OF EMAIL COMMUNICATION

Wordiness is probably the biggest sin of email and all written communication. The confident writer uses not formal, fussy language but Plain English which makes their writing clear, brief and to-the-point.

Most of us receive too many emails. That's a given. But what specifically irritates you about how emails are written?

Participants in my Business Writing workshop list their email pet hates. In this article we reveal the top five complaints and what you can do about it. Be part of the solution, not part of the problem.

Complaint #1. Not Being Concise

Review your email draft with this question in mind, 'What unnecessary words can I delete?' Less is more. You can probably remove as much as 20 per cent of the words, yet your message will stand out even more clearly. Many people go into long-winded explanation or justification that takes up their reader's time.

Ask yourself, 'Is this sentence essential'. Delete those that are not.

Five Sentences

If possible, aim to get your message across in just five sentences.

After writing your email, count the number of sentences, then decide which unnecessary sentences can go.

Eventually you'll automatically stop 'waffling' and keep it to the essential five. And when you get good at doing it in five, aim for three!

Shorten Long Sentences

Long sentences make an email appear wordy.

To improve readability, here's a quick trick. Locate each time you write 'and', combining two ideas. Assess if it could just as easily be two sentences. Add a full stop or period to end the first sentence; start a fresh sentence where the 'and' would have been. To grasp each idea one at a time helps your reader follow your train of thought.

Complaint #2. Not Being Clear

Communication involves a sender and a receiver. Good communicators consider their recipient. They review their draft to remove any ambiguities or idea gaps.

Three Questions

Here are three questions you can ask yourself after writing your email draft:

1. Is there enough information for the recipient to act?
2. If proposing a time-based event like a meeting, have I listed my own availability as a starting point?
3. When requesting action, have I included a timeframe, when it's needed by? Email is full of unrealistic demands where everything is urgent. Good time management is about working to priority. Stating a timeline aids that.

Complaint #3. Re-Using Old Subject Headers

Frequently mentioned as a major irritation is using superseded subject headers when the topic has changed. It can lead to confusion or your email being missed altogether.

Know When To Pick Up The Phone

If you find yourself rewriting the same paragraph over and over or struggling to find just the right words, there's a 50/50 chance your email will be misunderstood. Consider picking up the phone.

Complaint #4. Negative Tone

A live conversation over the phone or face to face is two-way. You can amend what you say based on responses you receive. Email is a monologue. Without the benefit of tone of voice or facial expression to soften what you are saying, words on their own in an email might be perceived as brusque or rude, (despite that not being your intention).

Tone: Command vs Possibility

A Customs Officer writing to an importer might include, 'You must comply with the law by. . .' But consider the use of 'You must comply with the law by . . .' Does that sound officious?

What if they write instead, 'Please comply with the law by . . .'? Does that get the same idea across without sounding heavy-handed?

Here Are 'Command' Words To Avoid In Business Writing:

- must
- should
- ought to
- have to
- need to
- required to

Instead Replace With The Language Of Possibility:

- I recommend or It is recommended that . . .
- Would you be willing to . . .
- Please . . .
- You might like to . . .
- If you can . . . it would be appreciated.

Complaint #5. No Salutation

Are you too busy to write *'Dear'* or *'Hello'*, or better, *'Good morning'* or *'Good afternoon'* followed by your recipient's name? I suggest you are too busy not to. Relationships are what make a team hum. Did you know some people not only notice lack of a salutation, but in fact are offended by that omission? It may not be important to you, but it's important to *them*.

I personally prefer 'Good morning' or 'Good afternoon' and their name. It's courteous, it adds positive tone and endears the reader. As well, adding a simple 'Hope you are well' after the salutation takes only a second to add, and does wonders for adding positive tone.

Don't Blame

Before accusing anyone, don't assume. Ask a question instead. And the best response when you receive a negative email? Don't justify or explain. Reply simply with a sincere, 'Let's do coffee and talk about it.'

TOP 5 BUSINESS WRITING MISTAKES AND HOW TO FIX

Here are the top five business writing mistakes. Are you making any of these?

Mistake #1. Sentences And Paragraphs Too Long

Limit sentences to maximum 22 words, paragraphs to four or five lines, and short reports and documents to one page (rarely two). If you can't say it well on one page, you probably can't say it well at all.

Mistake #2. Using The 'I' Word Too Often

Some written communication may contain as many as 20 or 30 uses of 'I', but communication shouldn't be all about the writer. Rewrite your sentence with a reader-focus, starting 'you' rather than 'I'. For example:
You will receive . . . vs I will send you . . .

Mistake #3. Using Formal Register

'Enclosed herewith please find . . . ' This sounds formal and stuffy. You don't talk that way, do you? Business communication uses what's called standard register (or style), not formal register. Write the way you speak (without becoming too informal).

Mistake #4. Run-On Sentences And Comma-Splices

I like chocolate ice-cream she likes vanilla.

This example is actually two sentences in one. Adding a comma after 'ice-cream' does not fix the problem. In fact, we then have another common error, a comma-splice. A comma alone cannot join two complete sentences.

Solution #1. Keep the comma and add a connecting word.
I like chocolate ice-cream, but she likes vanilla.

Solution #2. Join with a semi-colon.
I like chocolate ice-cream; she likes vanilla.

Mistake #5. Using Passive Voice Instead Of Active

Consider this sentence: The chair was broken by Jim.
This is an example of passive voice.
Compare with active voice: *Jim broke the chair.*

In active voice, Jim performs the action. But in passive voice, the chair is being acted upon.

The email was written by him. Passive.
He wrote the email. Active.

Dynamic active voice:
- uses fewer words
- is to the point
- sounds better
- reads better.

Action

A clue to finding passive voice in your writing, search your document for the word 'by'; for example,

- The report was sent by . . .
- The meeting was chaired by . . .

To transform active to passive, simply turn it around:

- The Registrar sent the report . . .
- The Team Leader chaired the meeting . . .

ANATOMY OF A
CUSTOMER-FRIENDLY EMAIL

Because an email is relying 100% on words to communicate without the benefit of facial expression or tone of voice, the words you choose can influence decisions and make a difference. Here are some tips for customer-friendly email writing.

1. Always Open With a Super Positive Salutation.

'Dear' or *'Hello'* is just ok. In a previous chapter I suggested starting with *'Good morning'* or *'Good afternoon'* plus their name? This adds positive tone right from the start.

Whichever salutation you use is part of branding, affects client perception and should be consistent throughout the organisation.

2. If It's Possible To Start With a Thank You, Start With Thank You.

- 'Thank you for your invoice.'
- 'Thank you for your email.'
- 'Thank you for your update.'

Starting with a thank you adds positive tone and enhances a relationship.

3. Whenever Any Action Is Requested, Embed 'Please' In The Question.

Which reads better?

'Please amend the billing name on all future invoices.'

vs

'Could the billing name be amended on all future invoices?'

In the second example, 'please' is missing. It sounds more officious, even reprimanding. It can put the reader off-side.

Your choice of words talks to your reader. It's called the writer's voice. In literature, Ernest Hemingway's voice is different to Patrick White which is different to James Joyce.

In the world of business, client emails have a voice too. Every email you send is a moment of truth, that is, customers make a decision about whether it's easy and pleasant to do business with you (or not).

No message is neutral. You are either enhancing your organisation's perception or detracting. If it's too wordy, if there's no white space in the layout, if tone is too robotic and distant, it influences your client perception.

Consider the business voice in this opening of an email in the Standard Style, *'We are in receipt of invoice number . . . '*

This style is what authors of the book, *The Cluetrain Manifesto*[1], call 'robo-voice'. *Cluetrain* authors urge us to write instead with a human voice.

On my bookshelf next to my copy of *Cluetrain* is an antiquarian book, *The Companion Letter Writer* published by F. Warne & Co.[2]

One of its business letter-writer template responses starts with *'We are in receipt of . . . '* What year was it published? Answer: 1866. If your communication still uses *'We are in receipt of . . . '*, it's not just last century, but in fact, century-before-last.

Your correspondence is your organisation's image, branding and perception. If you wouldn't say it like that over the phone, don't write it in an email. Write the way you speak (without becoming too informal).

POOR GRAMMAR AND SPELLING COSTS BUSINESS BILLIONS IN LOST SALES

Did you know 30% of customers won't buy from businesses that use poor spelling and grammar?

A Royal Mail survey[3] of 1,000 consumers in the UK showed that poor grammar, spelling and layout costs businesses billions in lost sales.

- 74% of customers distrust businesses using poor spelling or grammar
- 30% say they won't buy any product or service from them

According to the survey, companies who failed to invest in training their staff in grammar and spelling lost customers and revenue.

Good written communication, however, opens doors and wins deals. Alex Batchelor, Royal Mail's Director of Marketing said, 'Businesses are losing the goodwill and faith of customers by failing to pay attention to good English.[4] This study is proof that poor communication really does hit companies where it hurts — the bottom line.'

Batchelor continued, 'Now we know it has a financial impact. Customers are just driven away.

'No business is perfect but we recognise the need for all employers to encourage staff to actively check documents going out to customers.' The survey also revealed that only 56% of workers rely on the spellcheck function to proof their business documents. This function could be used more.

Why Is Writing Now So Important?

In the 60s, telephones dominated business communication. It was easier to pick up the phone than pen a letter. With email, writing has made a comeback. It's more important than ever to write with impact and clarity.

If you think about the number of times your people have to write something in a typical week, and every communication reflects your company image . . . scary, isn't it? Grasping the secrets of good English usage gives your business a competitive advantage. It's powerful.

TO REDUCE WORDINESS, USE ACTIVE VOICE

Business readers prefer direct and concise writing, using as few words as possible. Did you know you can reduce the number of words used overall by as much as 30% by using active voice? Here's an example:

- *John hit the ball.'* (four words) — active voice takes the form of 'A does B'.
- *'The ball was hit by John.'* (six words) — passive voice takes the form of 'B is done by A'.

How To Spot

Tell-tale compound verbs like *'were ordered', 'was written'* are clues to passive voice. Often there is an extra preposition, usually *'by'*, for example. *'The house was built by Smith Brothers'.*

You can quickly search for every occurrence of a specific word or phrase using your document's 'find' function.

Re-read the sentences one of these words appears and if it is in passive voice, recast the sentence in active voice. You will reduce the number of words and make the tone more confident, direct and energetic.

Tip: do a word count before and after this process to determine how many words you were able to delete, simply by switching from passive to active voice.

When Is Business Writing Too Abstract?

Using nouns instead of verbs makes writing abstract and hard to read. It's called nominalisation, and too much of it is a bad thing.

Compare the sentence, *'They conducted an investigation.'* with *'They investigated it.'* The first sentence doesn't have nearly as much impact as the second, does it?

Avoid changing verbs into nouns. Use the verb more often; it's more dynamic.

- instead of, *'We made a decision.'* write *'We decided.'* That's vigorous English.
- 'We reached an agreement.' is better expressed as 'We agreed.'
- for 'The introduction of . . . ' use 'By introducing . . . '
- ' . . . to submit an application . . . ' becomes ' . . . to apply for . . . '
- instead of ' . . . *conduct an assessment* . . . ' simply use ' . . . *assess* . . . '

In summary, a simple step for clearer writing is to use more verbs, fewer nouns.

Action

Locate any abstract nouns in your writing and turn them back into verbs. Clues to look for? Look for words ending in -ion, -tion, or -ment.

HOW TO GAIN EMAIL CUT-THROUGH FOR QUICKER RESPONSE

Are you ever frustrated waiting for an email response? You can't move to the next step in a project because action you've requested by email hasn't been completed? Do you simply resend the same email again and again?

Many of us have email inboxes that are overfull. How can you grab your recipient's attention if they are swamped by a deluge of emails? Here are some creative ways to gain attention and get done the action you need.

1. Pick Up The Phone Instead

It's hard for someone to ignore a living, breathing human at the end of the phone line. Don't simply resend the email. Pick up the phone instead.

Voicemail

And if you dial and get their voicemail, don't overwhelm them with detail. Here's the best message to leave. I call it the QQ (quick question) message:

'Hi [their name].

This is [your name].

I have a quick question for you.

Please call me on [your number].'

Curiosity about the quick question forces them to call.

2. Subject Line

If a phone call still doesn't inspire action, what can you do to make your next email stand out?

Answer. Put urgency language in the first word of the subject line. Here's a list to choose from:

- Action requested: (Sounds better than 'Action required'.)
- Reminder:
- Resending:
- Did you miss this?
- Urgent:
- Important:

Busy people appreciate a visual indicator in the subject line so they know what to action first.

3. Set A High Importance Level

To indicate the message needs the recipient's attention, you can set the level of importance as high. Recipients see a visual indicator — a red exclamation mark — in their inbox. You'll find this function in the 'Options' group.

4. Use Fewer Words

Can you reduce your email to three or five sentences? Wordy emails get ignored. Concise emails get actioned.

5. Give A Reason

Check any email requests that are being ignored. Is it lacking a reason you are making that request? Add the reason; watch the responses come in.

People are influenced when a reason is given with a request for action. For example, 'Because our client is asking for an answer . . . '

6. Attach A Read Receipt Request

A read receipt request makes the recipient feel like you are 'watching' for their response. But don't attach a read receipt request with every email you send though. Email users often mention this feature as a source of irritation. Use read receipt sparingly.

7. CC: Their Supervisor

Warning. *Be very careful.* You are now escalating the situation over their head. Know the right time to bring in a supervisor so you don't destroy trust or be regarded as a snitch.

8. And If All Else Fails, Phone Their Supervisor

Another warning. I don't need to remind you, *this is a last resort.*

In summary . . . What tactics do you use to gain faster response to your emails? What's working for you?

DON'T HIDE BEHIND EMAIL. KNOW WHEN TO PICK UP THE PHONE.

Composing an email, ever found yourself writing and rewriting the same paragraph over and over, struggling to find just the right words to convey the correct tone? That's a sure sign to pick up the phone instead.

We are so used to communicating through email; do we sometimes hide behind it? So how do you know when to pick up the phone rather than email?

Here Are Three Scenarios:

1. You want to influence someone to say 'yes' or there's no response to a request; pick up the phone.

2. A deadline looms and you wish to remind them of the urgency; pick up the phone.
3. You have to convey negative or disappointing news; pick up the phone.

Words alone lack the additional meaning that comes from tone of voice, facial expression, body language and other non-verbal cues. This means when writing emails it makes sense to include words that add conscious positive tone and friendliness. For example, you can start with a friendly opening such as:

- Hope you are well.
- Thank you for your email.
- How are things?

If a friendly phrase is absent, your email might sound abrupt.

Any request, make sure the word 'please' is included. (You'd be surprised how often that magic word is missing.) Rock musician and humanitarian, Bob Geldof, once said during a conference presentation, 'an ill-considered email can destroy a deal.'[5]

Consider the attributes of a phone call:

1. It's a dialogue. (Email is a monologue.)
2. You don't have to say everything you are thinking all at once.
3. You can monitor or adjust what you say, even as you speak, based on your listener's reactions. Even non-verbal sounds ('Oo', 'Hmm', 'Oh') tell you something.
4. Your own vocal tone influences how the message is received.
5. With email there's a lag between when you send, when it's read, and when you read their reply. Confusion or ambiguity can fester during this limbo period. With a phone call, you can generally tell if you're getting your message across.

Case Study

As a PR exercise, an accounting firm decided to post all clients a letter informing them about upcoming changes to tax law. So clients could take appropriate and timely action, this information was useful only if mailed well before end of the financial year.

Instead of a face-to-face Planning Meeting explaining the benefit to clients and to the firm, generating enthusiasm for the extra effort involved, an email was sent to administration staff informing them they would be doing this mailout.

They were not asked, 'Would you be willing to assist our firm raise our profile with our clients?' No perception of choice.

Guess what happened. The email and its reminder were simply ignored by recipients until the last minute when there was a mad rush to complete the mailout (which included an 'all hands on deck' weekend shift).

With any special project, first win the hearts and minds of the people involved. It's hard to lead an extra effort through email alone. Know when the power of influence is better gained face-to-face or over the phone.

COMMAS MADE SIMPLE WITH FANBOYS

In business writing we urge people to be aware if sentences are too long. Conversely, short isolated sentences make writing 'choppy', for example: *The machine broke down. The operator fixed it. Now it runs well.*

Good writing connects short sentences into one complex sentence, correctly punctuated. *The machine broke down, so the operator fixed it. Now it runs well.*

What are called 'joiner' words allow writers to join sentences to eliminate choppiness.

'FANBOYS' is a handy acronym to help remember the seven joiner words you can use with a comma to splice two sentences. 'And' and 'But' are the most common of the seven joiner words and here is the list of seven:

F — FOR
A — AND
N — NOR

B — BUT
O — OR
Y — YET
S — SO

The trend today is towards fewer commas, so it's not essential to place a comma before a joiner word, but it is still correct if you choose to.

Action: Remember the acronym FANBOYS as a memory aid for when it's correct to place a comma.

An exception

If the sentence fragment coming after the 'fanboys' joiner word is NOT a sentence, do not use a comma.

- I enjoyed the movie and want to see it again.
- The storm raged but didn't spoil our fun.

Action

Watch for complete sentences within sentences and use a FANBOYS comma to join them.

Present
persuasively

Presentation literacy isn't an optional extra for the few.
It's a core skill for the twenty-first century.

Chris Anderson, Curator, TED talks

FIVE COMMON PRESENTING MISTAKES

Wages are higher for job-seekers with presentation skills ability. The Foundation for Young Australians analysed 4.2 million online job postings from 2012 to 2015 in Australia from more than 6000 sources to uncover what employers are looking for. Roles requesting presentation skills paid many thousands of dollars more per year.[1]

Most people underestimate the power of being a good presenter. Speaking well in front of your team has the ability to make you come across as poised, confident and competent.

Here are five common presenting mistakes to avoid.

1. *Pacing Back And Forth*

If your way of coping with nerves is to stalk back and forth like a caged cat, your audience will get so distracted they'll be more interested watching you wear a path in the rug than in what you have to say. Maintain a positive stance, make good eye contact and smile. Then when you do move, you'll look and feel natural.

2. *Weak Opening And Closing*

The first 90 seconds are crucial. In fact, the first seven seconds are even more crucial. We form a first impression in the blink of an eye. Author, Malcolm Gladwell, refers to thin-slicing.[2] The audience makes judgements even before you speak. Think about how you move, how you take your position in front of the group, your eye contact, whether you are smiling and appear confident, how you deliver your first line.

Memorise your opening sentence so it's powerful, clear, and confident. You'll gain your audience's undivided attention which breeds self-confidence. Then you're on your way to a competent performance.

A strong close should include a review of your key ideas and a call to action. Then your audience will remember the important points you made and perhaps be inspired to take action.

3. Lack Of Structure

Simply put, tell your audience at the start what you are going to tell them, tell them, and then tell them what you just told them. Make sure you plan and rehearse a structure; a beginning, middle and an end.

Storyboard

One way to plan your structure into a logical flow is to storyboard it.

1. Start by listing of all your key ideas. (Writing by hand in a notepad may assist idea generation because it accesses a different part of the brain.)
2. Transfer each idea onto a post-it note or index card, in any order. Alternatively, create Word table document, 16 equal boxes per page, as many pages as needed. Type each idea into centre of each box. Print out the document, then cut each box into separate notes.
3. Use one large sheet of paper or cardboard as a flat surface to lay out all your idea notes. Re-arrange in any order that seems logical.
4. Stick or staple each note in the order you decided. You now have a storyboard!
5. Display your storyboard as your visual planner, and feel proud you've achieved this milestone!

Use the Storyboard method to plan a presentation, book, blog article, film or video, any project or special event — anything with a beginning, middle and end.

4. Weak Gestures

It builds rapport with your audience to let your hands talk as you present, using definite gestures. In fact, the most popular TED Talks are with speakers who use a ton of gestures[3] e.g. author/speaker Simon Sinek is one great example. Keep your hands above the waist and feel free to extend your arms away from your body. Alternate between one hand and two hand gestures. Avoid pointing though; it sub-consciously registers as aggressive. Barack Obama popularised the thumb on top of a closed fist; so that's safe to emulate.

5. Not Rehearsing Til You Know It

Being able to present is a life skill. When you present it's you, in front of your audience, whether it's two people or two thousand. You owe it to yourself to do the best you can do, having done the preparation. Don't just wing it.

All successful actors study their craft. On a good day, their natural talent takes over. On a bad day, when they're not feeling 100%, they fall back on their craft to deliver a superlative performance based on years of training.

Similarly with presenting. Rehearse, but don't memorise, (apart from your opening line to get you started.) Each time you rehearse, expect the flow of ideas to change a little. That's natural. It shows you are navigating intuitively through the content; which is exactly what you want to do during the presentation.

As a case in point, I was booked for an interview for a business podcast. Ahead of time, and to help me prepare, the host sent sample questions. As well, I listened to a few episodes so I would be acquainted with the format. Two days before the recording I rehearsed with my assistant asking the same questions.

During rehearsal I wasn't satisfied with my responses, so we crafted bullet points of my preferred answers. An hour before the interview, like an actor 'getting into character', I switched off my phone, and primed my brain for the interview to come. Because I'd 'done the work', the right words came out in the right order and logical flow. I was speaking with authenticity and without notes.

Do the work and the words will flow, off the cuff, in a natural way, so you can speak from the heart.

FIVE COMMON
SLIDESHOW MISTAKES

Mistake #1. Relying Too Much On Your Slideshow

Have you ever attended a presentation where the speaker actually read from the slides? Did you find it boring, or even irritating? Multimedia should support your presentation; it shouldn't *be* the presentation.

Use cue cards with keywords and rehearse until you know it. Then rely on memory to convey your message. (You can have your cue cards nearby to refer to, but if possible, put them aside and out of your hands.)

I do not recommend memorising your presentation. Just be natural, be conversational, be human and . . . trust yourself!

Presenter View in PowerPoint® allows you to see the upcoming slide as a trigger for the next piece of content. If you have a printout on paper of all your slides with the number of each slide clearly marked, then if you do want to quickly switch to a future slide, you can simply type in the number, hit enter and voila, that slide displays! (Refer to the later chapter on PowerPoint® keyboard shortcuts.)

Mistake #2. Too Many Words Per Slide

The current trend is for slides to display fewer words. Use a strong photo with one key word or short phrase and let what you say be off the cuff. After all, you are the expert. Never, ever read out the words off a slide.

If you do have to display words on a slide, aim for a maximum of six keywords per slide. This keeps the font to readable size for those who forgot their glasses. The slides are there to *support* your message, not merely repeat or *be* the message.

The audience has better memory of your information if they are not distracted by having to switch off listening to you to read a wordy slide.

Mistake #3. All Text, No Visuals

Use slides to reinforce your message with visuals conveying emotion. For example, if you were presenting on pollution, a photo of an oil-covered bird or a city clouded by smog conveys the message emotionally, while you might still discuss EPA data and statistics.

Tip: Use good quality stock photos rather than clipart. For a small outlay a stock photo looks more professional, less 'cheesy'. And get in the habit of taking your own photos you can use on slides.

Mistake #4. Using Too Many Transitions, Spins, Wipes, Dissolves

Use transition devices and sound effects sparingly. Less is more.

Mistake #5. Dimming the Lights So Your Face Is In The Dark

The purpose of a presentation is to communicate with your audience. People are engaged by eye contact and facial expression. Aim to connect with the people in front of you. Let them see the sparkle in your eye. Facial expression and body language is 55% of communication, tone of voice and words combined are only 45% of the total message.

HOW TO GRIP AN AUDIENCE FROM YOUR FIRST LINE

If I open a presentation with a thought-provoking question or startling fact, such as . . .

'Do you know what's really scary about India? The population is 1.3 billion people, yet 35% are under 15 years of age.'[4]

This question and answer construct is dramatic and has impact. What if I'd opened my talk instead with . . .

'Today I'm going to talk about the population growth in India.'

If you were in the audience, your response would probably be . . . (yawn), ho hum.

There are many ways to open a presentation, and my personal favourite is to ask a provocative question relevant to the topic. Four simple adjectives evoke a visceral, emotional response. Those four words are:

- weird
- scary
- hard
- stupid.

I acknowledge Judy Carter, author of *The Comedy Bible*, who taught me the 'four attitudes'.[5]

Put one of those words in a question, pause, then answer the question with an amazing fact, and you've got an opening that's dramatic and has impact!

For example:

'Do you know what's really stupid about distributing our product catalogue to letterboxes in December every year?'

(Pause)

'In the first two weeks of December, our catalogue is competing with 16 million other catalogues distributed at that time!'

Here's the construction again:

- question
- pause
- statement

For example:

'Do you know what's really scary about Customer Service?'

(Pause)

'The more you raise the bar, the more customers expect!'

This formula may not work with all of your material all of the time, but it probably works with some of your material some of the time. And when it does work, it creates impact.

How To Make It Work

1. Avoid making a single statement that both asks and answers the question. For example, avoid this:

    'Did you know it's scary our website attracts three million visitors every year but only 3% make a transaction?'

    That construction is weak and does not have impact. Remember . . . it's question — pause — statement. Here's the same idea again, this time using the construction, question — pause — statement:

    'Do you know what's really scary about our website?'
    >(Pause)
    'It attracts 3 million visitors a year, yet only 3% of them make a transaction!'

2. Avoid drawing attention to the question with a lead-in statement like *'I'd like to ask you a question . . .'* Go straight in, ask the question, be dramatic. You might like to open this way even before you introduce yourself or overview what your talk will be about.

3. Avoid the temptation to use a quality other than *weird, scary, hard* or *stupid*.

    'Do you know what's really amazing about . . .' does not create the same effect as, 'Do you know what's really stupid about . . .'

    Weird, scary, hard, stupid are four words with attitude! And once you've asked your question, paused, and answered it, then relax, drop the dramatics and perhaps go on with . . .

    'Hi, my name is <name>, and today we're going to discover . . .'

In closing, do you know what's really weird about asking a question using *weird, scary, hard* or *stupid* to open a presentation? The more you take a risk with a provocative question, the more impact you have with your audience!

HOW TO DITCH YOUR NOTES AND SPEAK WITH CONFIDENCE

When preparing to present, write it out, make cue cards, rehearse, but once in front of your audience, trust yourself to remember.

Let me tell you a story about how I learned to avoid coming across as stiff or wooden when presenting. I was asked to deliver five minutes on my usual subject, not to a workshop of 16 people, but to an after-dinner audience of 80 people. This was out of my comfort zone.

Rather than rehearsing my five minutes over and over til I was confident, instead I relied on creating good notes on cue cards. I took my beloved notes with me onstage; and my notes became my master. Instead of focusing on audience reaction, engaging them with eye contact, I became a slave to 'getting it right'.

The outcome? I appeared nervous, uncomfortable, lacking in confidence, in a word — wooden. Upon reflection, I vowed forevermore to rehearse til I knew it, then trust myself to speak off the cuff.

It's All About Self-Trust

In an extreme sport like skydiving, there's a motto — *check your equipment, then trust your equipment.* When presenting, prepare, write it out, make cue cards, rehearse. But once in front of your audience, trust yourself, (trust your sub-conscious). Put your notes aside.

So What If You Forget A Detail?

Firstly, your audience doesn't know what you forgot to say. Secondly, if what you omitted was essential to understanding, and if you allow time for Q&A, a question allows you to respond confidently and appear the expert.

Don't Memorise

Have you discovered when rehearsing that each time you deliver there's a different logical flow? If so, that's good. It means you are navigating intuitively through your content. Let go and allow it to unfold.

Be Extemporaneous

This word comes from the Latin, *ex tempore*, meaning 'out of the moment'. To speak extemporaneously is to speak off the cuff, in a smooth, dynamic way, without the aid of notes.

How To Be Extemporaneous

You wouldn't use your slideshow as your notes, would you? Research shows when a speaker reads aloud the same text displayed on a slide it not only annoys and frustrates an audience, it also interferes with recall. That one behaviour not only contributes to your coming across as 'wooden', it also reduces your credibility.

Make your slides a visual feast. Find an emotive photo image, add a single keyword and move away from slides full of text.

Don't Use Notes

If you let go of notes, your words will follow an organic flow and you will be more personally engaging. You will also appear more confident, poised and professional.

But don't memorise. With learning it all off by heart, there's a danger again of sounding hollow.

It can make you stiff or wooden. Rehearse at least one complete run-through within 24 hours of the event, then let go and trust yourself to navigate intuitively through your content.

The purpose of being 'in the flow' is to sound natural and appear authentic. It gives you freedom to focus on your audience, make eye contact and connect with the room.

Eye Contact

It has been suggested that to avoid nerves, stare over the heads of your audience to look at the back wall. That's misinformation! Good eye contact is engaging and inclusive.

As you express one idea or sentence, maintain eye contact with a member of your audience. Then shift eye contact to a new person and continue with the next new idea or sentence.

Eventually each member of the audience will be the point of your focus at least once. You can also use the 'Z' — sweep your eyes at a moderate pace, in 3 sweeps — Back row, left corner to right corner, to front row, left corner, to front row right corner.

Then do it again, sweeping your eyes in a slightly different Z motion, eyes landing on a different person each time.

Cue Cards vs Notes

If notes are a safety net, what style of notes are acceptable to an audience without affecting your perception as an authority on your topic? Full page notes allow you to write full sentences. That's ok during preparation. But once you have your written-out text, move to system cards or palm cards. Rewrite your notes as keywords to trigger memory.

Content vs Process

Have you ever encountered a speaker who, when told they have five minutes remaining, simply speeds up and firehoses the content? When a speaker speeds up, do listeners think faster? More likely they mentally switch off, waiting for it all to end!

Remember, content is not more important than process. When running out of time, simply draw easily to a natural conclusion, still leaving time for Q&A.

Master Self-Talk

How you mentally speak to yourself before you go on has an effect. Observe what you say to yourself, and replace a negative thought, such as 'What if I forget thing?' with a positive affirmation such as, 'I know enough to be successful.'

Action

- Instead of full page notes, transfer keywords to cue cards.
- Practice, rehearse, know it so well you can drop cue cards altogether.

- Don't memorise by rote. Navigate intuitively through the content.
- Master self-talk. Tell yourself, 'I know enough to be successful', and 'people will like me'.

WHY YOU SHOULD STEER YOUR PRESENTATION WITH MORE QUESTIONS

Do you ask lots of questions when you present? Don't tell; remember to ask instead.

Why Ask Questions?

When you ask a question, your audience seeks out the answer in their own minds. The lights literally go on in their brains (brain scans illustrate this). Automatically, your audience is more engaged and actively listening.

'Why is it so?' became a household phrase in Australia and North America from the sixties to the eighties due to Physicist, Professor Julius Sumner Miller's appearances on TV demonstrating intriguing mysteries of physics.

He would ask questions such as:

- How tall a mirror do you need to see all of you?
- What would happen if there were no friction in the world?
- How do waves break?

The Professor's goal was 'to stir interest, awaken enthusiasm, arouse curiosity, kindle a feeling, fire up the imagination.'[6]

Here are suggestions about how to ask an intriguing question:

1. Instead of going straight in with, *'John P. Kotter says about Change Management . . .'* preface your statement with a leading question such as, *'What do the experts say?'*

2. Rather than, 'The Australian Bureau of Statistics report on . . . ' you can pose, 'Where can we find evidence for this?'
3. Instead of assuming, 'I'm sure you read the article this week about . . . ' ask, 'Did you see the article this week about . . . ?'
4. Rather than the assumption, '*You all know Amazon dot com*', query, '*Who is familiar with Amazon dot com?*' In any group, it's possible one person is not familiar with something the other 99% are.
5. Instead of telling, 'Here's what you can do', ask, 'How can you make a difference?'

How To Start A Question

Consider Rudyard Kipling's poem[7]:

I keep six honest serving-men
(They taught me all I knew);
Their names are What and Why and When
And How and Where and Who.

These six questions — who, what, where, when, why and how — are known as the 'journalist's credo'. In journalism the six Ws (the sixth word ends in 'w') are regarded as essential to information-gathering. Use these six words to spice up your presentation with more questions.

Open With A Question

You can capture your audience's attention by opening with a dramatic question:

- Do you know what's really scary about . . . ?
- Have you ever wondered why . . . ?

Segue Questions

Questions are useful segues — (pronounced 'seg-way') — devices to move a speaker smoothly to the next section or theme of a presentation.

For example, '*Now that I've* . . . [explained how Customer Relationship Management works] . . . *the question remains,* [what frequency is just right for staying in touch with clients]*?*'

Rhetorical Questions

A rhetorical question is asked for effect; an answer is not expected.

When Mark Antony in Shakespeare's play, Julius Caesar, asked, *Was this ambition?'*, he meant it as a rhetorical question. Bob Dylan's song 'Blowin' in the Wind' is full of rhetorical questions, *'How many roads must a man walk down before you call him a man?'*

In a presentation, add rhetorical questions.

Thought-Provoking Questions

You can conclude your talk with a startling question to get people thinking and talking. For example:

'Suppose you were given the opportunity to send three small items and a short message in a deep-space probe that might be found by aliens . . . What would you send? What would your message be?'

A question like that will send your listeners on a mental journey seeking the answer.

Action

1. For any statements in your presentation, ask yourself, 'How can I restate this as a question?'
2. Identify segue transition points in your presentation and lead into the next section with a question.
3. Is there a question that would make a dramatic conclusion?

HOW TO HANDLE Q&A

When presenting to an audience, have you ever arrived at the end of your talk and, almost as an after-thought, asked feebly, 'Any questions?' (Perhaps you half-hoped they wouldn't ask any?)

Welcome Questions, They're Engaging

The biggest mistake presenters make is not allowing enough time for questions and answers (Q&A). Often your audience will ask what they are most interested to know.

Have you ever attended a live musical performance where the encore was actually the best part of the evening? Musicians usually plan what they will play in an encore. Still with five or ten minutes to go is a good time to open up to questions. If it tapers off, you can revert to bonus content, like a planned encore.

But if questions are lively and flowing, that's great. That's exactly what your audience wants or needs to hear. It's what they'll be talking about in the break.

Have A Seed Question Prepared

One way to get the ball rolling is to remark, *'One question I'm often asked is . . .* ' (One speaker tells me they write a starter question on an index card and briefs someone ahead of time, that if there is silence, to be ready to ask.)

Give Them Forewarning

Let them know shortly ahead of time by saying, 'In a few minutes, I'll open the floor to any questions you might have.'

When you arrive at a logical conclusion, use a palms-up gesture and mirror the words you used before, 'And now I'll open up the floor to any questions you might have.' Then pause, and make good eye contact. Look like you expect a question.

During Question-time, Here's A Few Tips:

1. Repeat The Question

It gives you time to think, to ensure you fully understand the question. And because you are facing them, everyone can catch what was said.

2. Take Your Time

Avoid responding too quickly to questions, even those you readily know the answer. That way you avoid bringing attention to one question difficult to answer compared to others you can answer quickly and easily.

3. Good Phrase To Use

'That's a good question', gives you time to think, while complimenting the person doing the asking. Remember to use this *one time only*.

4. Get To The Point

It's better to ask, 'Shall I say more on this?' than go into too much detail.

5. How To Check Understanding

Asking 'Do you understand?' puts the burden of comprehension on the listener. Instead, using 'Does that make sense?' suggests 'Have I explained it well?'.

DO YOU HAVE A CALL TO ACTION AT END OF YOUR PRESENTATION?

Whenever you present, even if your purpose is to inform rather than persuade or sell, you'll most likely want to connect with your audience.

One way to connect, and perhaps gauge how well your presentation was received, is to have a 'Call To Action' (CTA).

A simple CTA is to offer something free — for example, a free report or white paper — to anyone who gives you their business card at the end.

What if they don't have their business card with them?

Perhaps add a sticky note to every handout and ask them to write their name and email address to give to you.

You can even be a little creative.

We were consulting with a retail chain prior to their annual conference with franchisees. The goal of the Marketing Manager's presentation was to persuade franchisees to choose one of three point-of-sale opportunities to improve their store and benefit their customers. We devised a fun way to encourage people to make a commitment.

The presenter ended her talk with, 'Ladies and gentleman. Under your chair you will find three cards, green, purple and orange. The green card corresponds to Opportunity 1, purple card corresponds to Opportunity 2, orange card corresponds to Opportunity 3. Select the colour card which corresponds to the opportunity you'd like to participate. Please take it to my assistant, who will exchange it for a sample bag you can take away, filled with all the instructions you need to get started tomorrow.'

Measuring Success

You can use a Call To Action to measure success. If 20 out of 100 attendees give you their business card, that's a 20% response rate.

If you give the same talk at different locations, you can compare your results over time.

POWERPOINT® HACKS TO ADD SPARKLE TO YOUR SLIDESHOW

Ever seen a presenter position an object in front of a table projector to conceal a slide image beaming to the screen?

Would you like to know some easy PowerPoint® keyboard shortcuts that add sparkle to PowerPoint® and make you look more professional?

While presenting with PowerPoint®, have you ever wanted to digress for a moment from the topic displayed on the current slide and blank the screen? This is especially useful if you are asked a question that's off topic or simply to have a rest from light cast from the projector.

1. B and W Keys

- B Key
  Did you know when in Slide Show view there's a keyboard shortcut that immediately makes the screen blank? One key. Like magic. Gone to black! You can do this in one movement; the B key (B is for blank). And to resume, hit the B button again; your slide reappears. It's that simple.

- W Key
  Similarly, press the 'W' key to blank the screen white; press 'W' again and the slide reappears.

Knowing this keyboard shortcut allows you to be flexible when presenting. Your audience will find it refreshing to see you in control of your presentation; not PowerPoint® dominating you.

If you present and don't already know this shortcut . . . well, it will change your life! At least once during your presentation, shift your audience's attention from the visuals to the presenter by turning off your PowerPoint® slide to a blank screen.

Then when you are ready to go on, simply press the 'B' key again and your slide reappears.

And there it is —

B key to blacken the screen
W key to whiten the screen

2. Powerpoint® Help — Keyboard Shortcuts List

So what other keyboard shortcuts will make your life easier when you present? To see a list, when in Slide Show view, right click; a dialog box appears. Select Help and a list of keyboard shortcuts appear. Experiment with that list of functions.

3. 'Go To That Slide' Shortcut

Did you know you can go straight to any slide if you know its number? Type in its number followed by Enter. If you type Control key + S in Word, it saves; (in Mac it's Command key + S). But when you are in PowerPoint®

Slide Show, to see a list of slides, select Control + S to display a dialog box with all slides by number.

Avoid using ESC (escape Key) as it takes you out of PowerPoint®.

4. Hide Slide Shortcut

Have you ever wanted to modify a presentation, perhaps shorten it? Don't remove slides, hide them instead. Go into Slide Sorter View, right click on any slide you want to hide, a dialog box appears with 'Hide Slide' as an option.

Watch the slide number. As soon as you hide it, the number below the slide has a strikethrough line through it. Un-hide the slide with right click, select 'Hide Slide' again; it reverses the action.

5. Use A Wireless Remote

Avoid progressing slides by physically tapping the forward arrow on the keyboard with your finger. Instead, purchase a wireless presentation remote. This tool makes you look professional. You can stand anywhere in the room and progress to the next slide.

I presented a summary of these (and more) shortcuts at a national conference of professional trainers. At times I heard audible gasps from members of the audience (yes, professional trainers). A little know-how goes a long way to transforming how others perceive you as a speaker.

HOW TO BE PERCEIVED AS A POLISHED SPEAKER

Professionalism means understanding the unwritten ground rules of being part of an event when you are presenting. Here are some of the basics.

1. Print Your Intro On Paper And Hand to the MC

Nothing's worse than an MC reading out your profile verbatim off a website they found themselves. It's usually too long and often a little formal and not conversational in tone. Craft an interesting bio that engages the audience.

Email your intro ahead of time, and as well, bring it printed out on paper to hand to the MC. This one action oozes professionalism.

2. Arrive Early

Plan to be there early for sound check and setup. Find out ahead of time the scheduled break time prior to your session and plan to arrive then. Otherwise, up to 60 minutes early is good.

If there is a speaker before you, sit in and listen. A secret of professional speakers is to reference a point made by a previous speaker and connect it to their own topic.

3. Be Prepared

You may be expecting to use your own laptop only to find they ask for your slideshow on a USB flash drive. Always have your slideshow available on a drive. Even better, email it ahead of time so they can pre-load it onto the event laptop.

Bring a printout of your slideshow so that if technology fails it can be quickly photocopied as a take-away handout.

4. Be Nice To The AV Technician

The one person in the room who can make or break you is the one in charge of your slides, sound and lighting. There's no room for diva or divo behaviour (i.e. being temperamental or insisting on this or that).

5. Be Time-aware

Always finish on time; never go over time. If the previous speaker goes over time, ask the organiser if they want you to keep to the planned duration, or to condense your presentation so the schedule can get back to plan. It makes the whole event run smoothly if you can be flexible to shorten your talk to make up time . . . if they want you to. (Remember to ask and don't assume.)

Do you find it frustrating if a speaker announces, '*We've run out of time for questions*'?

It's good practice to open up to Q&A some minutes before the appointed end-time, to answer any burning questions. You may find it's the most engaging part of your talk. If running behind, be prepared to overview or summarise the rest, to end on time. And never ever speak faster to fit all your content in!

6. Don't Read Off The Screen

It used to be that a speaker could bumble along to a polite crowd, relying on a PowerPoint® slideshow featuring:

- bullet point
- bullet point
- bullet point

to convey their message. Not any more.

Today's audience is savvy and demand a higher level of engagement than ever before. Don't let the slideshow BE the presentation.

Why not prepare slides with a relevant photograph and keyword instead of the old text-based sea of words?

Here's an example. Talking about growth in city building construction? Show before and after photos of a city skyline; first image — without construction cranes; second image — same buildings, with construction cranes added.

7. Repeat The Question

Some people are hard of hearing, others just didn't catch it. Good practice is to repeat a question before answering. Not only is your audience grateful, but you have time to think before replying.

Action

Follow these seven tips and you'll demonstrate professional courtesy and respect whenever you are asked to present.

WHAT'S YOUR SELF-TALK BEFORE YOU SPEAK TO AN AUDIENCE?

Does your internal conversation sabotage your confidence just before you present? Let me tell you a story.

I was a contestant on a national TV quiz show. New contestants entered the set through sliding doors. Female contestants were accompanied by a male in formal attire. As he and I stood waiting for the sliding doors to open, he looked down at me and asked, 'Are you nervous?'

Perhaps he could have asked, 'How are you feeling?' or even, 'Do you feel confident?', (emphasising confidence rather than nerves). But no, he chose to ask, 'Are you nervous?', (focusing on nerves).

My answer was the positive affirmation I'd been saying to myself over and over like a mantra. I looked up at him and with a big smile declared, 'I feel supremely calm and confident.' (It may sound a little strange out loud, but quietly repeated to myself, it had been comforting and reassuring.)

What do you say to yourself before you present? Find a phrase that resonates with you. My phrase is 'I feel supremely calm and confident'. What's yours?

Action

1. Observe your self-talk, i.e. what you say to yourself leading up to and day of a presentation.
2. Substitute negative, self-limiting statements with positive uplifting ones.

Skyrocket your sales

DO YOU ASK ENOUGH DISCOVERY QUESTIONS WHEN SELLING?

Whether dealing with a customer or a colleague, it pays to ask questions before jumping to conclusions. No matter what your role, seek first to understand by asking questions. Questions help you avoid making incorrect assumptions.

What's the best way to handle an incoming sales enquiry over the phone? Do you open the conversation with a pitch, or do you take time to first discover their needs by asking questions? Do you take time to diagnose what is the real problem rather than rush into offer a solution too soon?

Most salespeople sell products rather than sell a solution. And the best way to diagnose a solution is to stay curious and ask powerful questions.

There's an art to phrasing questions.

In this article we'll explore the best way to create questions, how to ask them, including how to prime your brain before you even take that call, so you ask the right questions in the right order.

Why Ask Questions?

Questions are engaging. To answer a question requires your prospect to converse with you. It gets the conversational ball rolling and opens up the channels of communication.

Swiss psychiatrist and psychoanalyst, Carl Jung, (1875–1961), refers to 'positive transference'[1], the notion that once someone opens up about their problems or challenges, they direct positive feelings towards their listener, someone who 'understands'. This positive attachment means you become their trusted advisor; cultivates the hope that you will come through with a solution to their situation.

Avoid Talking 'At'

Offering a solution too soon often means you are talking 'at' people about your product or service; you're trying to get them to fit into your solution. But the moment you say, *'Tell me about the problem' or 'How long has that been happening?'* you demonstrate you want to get under the surface and truly understand the situation. You're cultivating the perception you'll come up with a tailored solution.

During that opening conversation you can ask, 'Does it make sense to look at the actual issues you want to solve first, then we can see if we're a good fit.' The impression you want to give is, 'I don't assume I can help you. Let's first find out what your challenges and issues are; then we can determine if we are a good fit.' Not only does that approach suggest you are not 'desperate' for the business, but also that you don't automatically say yes to every request for assistance.

This generates trust.

What Questions To Ask?

You might have heard about the difference between open and closed questions? A closed question is one where the answer is either yes or no. We sometimes fall into the trap of asking closed questions. But if you open the conversation with an open question such as, *'Tell me about why you've contacting us today,'* or *'Tell me about the challenges you're experiencing.'*

This approach is superior to greeting a prospect with a pitch.

Framing Questions

Don't just ask them, 'How long has this been going on?', add a pain word for emphasis, e.g. 'How frustrated are you by how long this has been going on?'

More Pain Words

Do you ever feel uneasy when . . . ?
Are you worried by . . . ?
Are you struggling to . . .?

These pain words emphasise the pain of not taking action, which leads to an opportunity to offer your solution down the track.

What-to-say Guide

I don't call it a script; I call it a what-to-say guide. Use a list of questions using conversational wording as a checklist to guide you through a diagnostic process.

And it is only a guide. Many times it feels right to ask questions out of the usual order and use whatever wording feels natural at the time.

Whether over the phone or face-to-face, prospects don't mind if you ask a series of 'get to know' questions. They feel listened to.

Over The Phone

My question checklist is a simple Word table, with a question in the left hand column, and space in the right hand column to insert the response. Using a headset to keep my hands free, I can simply type in the answers as they speak.

Face-to-face

If meeting in person, I take along a printout of my list of questions and handwrite the answers in the right hand blank column with a pen. (In the past I trialled, during face-to-face meetings, to type their answers directly onto my device. I felt a little silly, like I was typing a transcript of an interrogation. The handwritten document is the way to go; it feels more 'personal'.)

Action

1. Use conversational language.
2. Call it a 'diagnostic'.
3. It's okay to tell them you are writing notes as we go, so if they do decide to go ahead, you have it captured. Save these diagnostic notes in your client folder or CRM to refer to later.
4. To improve your chances of making the sale, summarise the key ideas and add it to your proposal.

One option — before sending your proposal — send first only their 'confidential brief'. You can ask them to confirm you captured it correctly. You are drip-feeding them your information which foreshadows the arrival of the proposal.

TOP 8 MISTAKES PEOPLE MAKE WHEN SELLING

Here are some errors people make when selling.

Mistake #1. Not Asking Enough Discovery Questions

Research shows a salesperson should encourage the prospect to speak, not even 50/50, but more than the salesperson!

By asking questions you're engaging your customer in a conversation. The worst thing you can do is to rush in with a solution and start telling your customer about your product.

Mistake #2. Being 'Busy' Instead Of Contacting Customers

One of the biggest mistake salespeople make is getting distracted by activity or 'being busy'. It might be spending time on a proposal or fulfillment of an order. Are you getting distracted from customer contact by secondary activities?

Call reluctance is being busy with other things other than picking up the phone to call a prospect because of some, often sub-conscious, emotional hesitation. Any time you're not talking to a customer — phone, face-to-face or email — you are not engaged in *income-generating* activities. If you notice a pattern of avoiding proactive customer contact, ask yourself, *'Am I suffering from* (what's known as) *call reluctance?'* And be honest with yourself.

The biggest pitfall for anyone involved in sales is convincing themselves that staying 'busy' leads to a sale. Customer contact leads to sales.

When it comes to drafting proposals, avoid perfectionism and get them out quickly so you can move forward to the next follow-up.

The 1 – 7 Method

One way to ensure you fit in your follow-ups is to decide on a number of contacts you're willing to commit to contacting, every business day, come what may. I work with seven.

At start of 'Sacred Contact Time', I write in my daybook numbers 1 through to 7, vertically, down the left hand side. Next I focus on contacting seven priority prospects — whether by email or phone.

If there are 20+ business days in a month, that's 140 touches. That keeps sales momentum going.

Mistake #3. Giving Up Too Soon

So many salespeople give up at the first '*no*' or '*we haven't had time to consider it yet.*'

A customer might need eleven touches — eleven contacts from you — before they say yes. If you give up and don't call back after touch number ten, you've lost the sale!

Stay In Touch During the Indecision Period

Sometimes it's all about timing. For some prospects, it's not '*no*' but '*not yet*'. If you stay in touch even when they tell you something else has come up, or we can't move forward, who will they think of when suddenly it comes back to being a priority?

Mistake #4. Not Describing 'WIIFM' — What's In It For Me

When mentioning a product feature it's important to also add, ' . . . what that means to you is . . . ' or ' . . . which means you won't ever have to . . . '

Remember to add the benefit every time you mention a feature of a product or service.

Mistake #5. Not Qualifying

Are you talking to the decision-maker? Are there multiple decision-makers? Remember to ask, '*Is there anyone else involved in making the decision?*' Offer to teleconference with all decision-makers.

(It might make sense to get your own web teleconference account for this purpose.)

Mistake #6. Not Managing Buyer Resistance

Create a what-to-say guide of replies to typical customer objections. Don't accept no; find ways to keep the conversation going.

Mistake #7. Not Asking For The Order

In this customer-savvy world, it's not about hard sell or asking closing questions any more.

A simple question like:

- 'So would you like to take the next step?'
- 'How would you like to move forward?'
- 'It makes sense to me to place an order, what do you think?'

posed at the right time can advance the sale and make a difference.

Mistake #8. Not Giving Post-sale Customer Service

Many salespeople get distracted by the next incoming enquiry and completely neglect a profitable area of repeat business — existing customers.

Existing customers are five to seven times more profitable than marketing to new customers. To forget about post-sale customer service is losing an opportunity to cross-sell, upsell and repeat sell.

WHEN IS THE BEST TIME TO CALL PROSPECTS?

To identify days of the week and times of day that generate highest connection rate, Boston-based Insight Squared analysed thousands of sales phone calls.[2]

Best Time

Their research pinpointed best time of day is between 10:00 am and 4:00 pm.

Once upon a time, conventional wisdom was to ring early, 8:00 am to 9:00 am, to reach decision makers before reception starts answering the phone. But these days, don't you find their voicemail is on? They won't pick up the phone at 8:00 am. And 9:00 am is still too early.

At 9:00 am the work day is starting in earnest. People are busy checking emails, meeting with staffers, getting the team rolling. People have to be receptive when you contact them, and research shows they're receptive between 10:00 am and 4:00 pm. So it's all in the timing.

Best Day

And best day of the week with the highest connect rate? Research indicates Tuesday. Wednesday is next best, followed by Monday, then Thursday, then Friday.

How can we apply this information?

If you are a business development professional, would you suggest a face-to-face meeting at their office on a Tuesday? If that's your best day to MAKE appointments, why would you be DOING appointments on that day? (Unless of course the client specifically requests that day for your meeting.)

Knowing Tuesday is the best contact day, preserve that day for in-office phone or email contact. Similarly, knowing Friday or Thursday are worse for reaching your prospect, schedule your out of office appointments on those days. You can orchestrate weekly activities around best days and times.

Case Study

Let me give you an example of how some salespeople, left unmonitored, do what they *feel* like doing, instead of doing what's best for getting results.

I was leading sales training in Melbourne with a telemarketing team and asked, *'What's the best time of day to connect with the people on your list?'* After discussion we settled on 10:00 am to 12:15 pm, then 2:15 pm to 04:15 pm.

I then asked, 'What time do you go to lunch?'

One staffer revealed she went to lunch after 2:00 pm each day. Why? Because she preferred lunch between 2:00 pm and 3:00 pm.

We went deeper.

'So, you're continuing to call prospects through the standard lunch hour, 1:00 pm to 2:00 pm, a time of day with a lower connect rate? Then at 2:00 pm, when people are coming back from lunch, that's when you take your lunch?'

By shining a light on unthinking, habitual behaviour she was able to see it was unproductive and commit to moving her lunch break forward.

Sacred Contact Time

In our business we make 9:00 am to 12:15 pm and 2:15 pm to 4:15 pm Sacred Contact Time. This means working with the calendar of scheduled follow-ups. And a follow-up may be a short nudge email or telephone call.

Outside of those times we fit in operational and admin tasks, compile proposals, or meet as a team. The key contact hours of the day are devoted to staying in touch with the people that matter, our valued prospects and clients.

So, what's true in your business?

Action

1. Analyse best days and times of day to reach prospects and clients by phone and/or email.
2. Does your sales team focus energy on contacting to best days and best times of day?
3. Display a sign, 'Sacred Contact Time', to focus attention and productivity.
4. Make a distinction between sales-generating behaviour and admin support tasks.

SALES HACK: WHAT IS THE BEST OPENING QUESTION?

Phoning a client, have you ever felt as if you were an interruption; it was something about their hurried pace or tone of voice? With email, your recipient chooses when to check their inbox, but a phone call is an interruption.

Therefore it's only courteous to first ask, before going into the reason for calling, *'Is this a good time to call?'* But consider what the response might be if you ask instead, *'Is this a bad time to call?'*

Good time vs *bad* time — which is better? Author Thomas Freese[3] recommends *'Is this a bad time to call'*, so I tried it. Yes, it works like a charm.

In marketing and in sales — test, test, test, test, test. If you ask *'Is this a good time to call?'*, you've left it open for them to reply, *'No it isn't. Can you call back another time please?'*. You've dialled but you haven't progressed the conversation, or the relationship. In sales this is what Neil Rackham, author of *Spin Selling*, calls a 'continuation'.[4]

Compare with, *'Is this a **bad** time to call?'* Even if it is an inconvenient time, you may find the likely response is, 'It's always a bad time, so go ahead anyway.' An advancement!

As a positive person, my natural inclination used to be to open a call with, *'Is this a **good** time to call?'* But after testing both versions, I'm now convinced, *'Is this a **bad** time?'* is more likely to gain a conversation then and there. This one little word change can make a big difference. Freese argues it taps into people's natural inclination to mismatch.

Regardless, if they can't accept your call then and there, remember to ask, *'When should I call back, please?'* When they respond with a time, you now have permission to phone back. An advancement.

This one sales hack, asking *'Is this a bad time to call?'* reduces phone tag, saves you time and unnecessary redialling, and ultimately advances the sale.

HOW TO RESPOND TO THE HOLLYWOOD BRUSH-OFF

Do you follow-up possible new clients after they request information? Here's an easy way to keep the door open to an ongoing relationship until the time is right for them to say 'yes'.

Perhaps you've experienced a possible new client shut the door to telephone follow-up with a brush-off statement like 'I'll contact you after

I've read your information.' That's what I call the Hollywood objection, 'Don't call us, we'll call you.' After auditioning, aspiring actors in Hollywood were often given this cliché response.

If you respond with, 'OK, I'll wait to hear from you then,' you haven't asked for permission to contact again.

Instead, use this 3-step method whenever you get a DCUWCU — don't call us, we'll call you — response, so you easily gain consent to stay in contact.

1. Say 'That's Fine.'

Your automatic reaction should be to agree by saying, 'that's fine.'

2. Ask Permission.

'And if I haven't heard from you in say, 10 days, is it ok to call you then?'

Start with 'and'; never use 'but' (which sounds oppositional and creates resistance.)

Judge the right timeframe. It might be one month or three months, whatever feels right.

Nine out of ten clients will say yes, unless they absolutely have zero interest and tell you again, 'No, please don't call.' That's good to know; you can simply take them off your call-back list.

3. When You Call Back, Remind Them They Gave You Permission.

'When we last spoke in < May >, you suggested I phone around this time regarding . . .' Now when they hear from you, you are not interrupting them, but following their instructions. This is the elegance of gaining permission.

How you end a sales call determines whether the next time you contact your prospect they'll be happy to hear from you or whether they'll consider your call an interruption.

Selling today is about continuously asking your customer for permission to stay in contact, so they expect to hear from you, keeping the door open to an ongoing relationship.

Action

1. Remember to end every phone call referring to the best timeframe to contact again, and wait for them to agree.
2. Then make sure you make a note of the agreed call-back date in client history and schedule the call-back on your calendar.

HOW TO CULTIVATE A VOICE PEOPLE TRUST

How important is your voice when selling? Do you build trust with a voice that displays energy, confidence and reassurance?

Does a high-achieving salesperson use their voice more effectively over the phone?

Salespeople with more inflection in their voices make more sales over the phone. A bright voice with energy and vocal variety is more persuasive than a boringly flat monotone.

How can we optimise our sales voice for the phone and become more polished in our vocal patterns? Let's consider these five vocal arts:

- inflection
- tone
- tempo
- pitch
- enunciation

1. Inflection

Inflection is the rise and fall of your voice when you speak. Imagine the sound of your voice drawn as a line graph.

A monotone forms a shallow wave line. A voice with energy and interest has a wider range, higher highs and lower lows.

Actors inflect all over the voice spectrum and have energy and drama in their voices.

What is your vocal range? Does your voice have energy?

Exercise 1

Here's an exercise to improve inflection.

Read a children's book aloud and over-inflect. Exaggerate it. The kids will love it, and you'll expand your vocal range at the same time. (The famous English thespian, Sir Laurence Olivier, as a rehearsal exercise, used to exaggerate words and actions of a script.)

Put more energy into it, inflect more, add more emotion and feeling.

2. Tone

'Selling is the transference of feeling', according to master sales trainer, Zig Ziglar.[5] But a voice with vocal variety is only half the equation.

It helps to believe in your product. Enthusiasm permeating your words adds emotional content.

One way to generate passion is to find a BIG REASON why your product or service benefits people.

For example, you are not simply selling stainless steel cookware, you are also improving people's health and wellbeing by moving them away from aluminium cookware to beneficial stainless steel.

Instead of simply selling stocks and shares, you are ensuring your client's financial future.

If you are only lukewarm about your product, that comes through when selling on the phone. Believe in the big picture benefit of your product so your passion shines through.

Exercise 2

Repeat the name of your organisation aloud in each of the following ways:

- angrily
- shyly
- laughingly
- despairingly
- passionately
- brightly

Did you notice there's a wide vocal range depending on the emotion?

Consider your voice as a musical instrument. And let enthusiasm and passion come through when speaking to clients.

3. Tempo

A branch of psychology called neuro-linguistic programming or NLP tells us that you create rapport when you actively listen and slow down or speed up to match the pace and style of the person you're talking to. So it's not whether your voice is too fast or too slow. Be flexible enough to speak a little faster or slower depending on the dialogue.

4. Pitch

Voices are high or low. Try humming a few bars of a simple song. That's your natural pitch. Now speak to clients in your natural pitch.

5. Enunciation

Do people not catch what you say and ask you to repeat? It could be you are mumbling and have poor diction.

To resolve this, open your mouth wider when speaking and pronounce your words more distinctly.

Do you drop your consonants? In the following sentence, make sure you emphasise the ends of words (in bold) so they can be heard:

'I'm wondering what you thought about the information I sent you?'

Good diction improves understandability, especially if you have a different regional accent.

Exercise 3

And if you observe you slur an occasional word, here's a simple exercise to fix that. Put your tongue in your cheek and say this tongue twister, 'red leather, yellow leather', once or twice each side.

6. Breathe

To increase his lung capacity for singing, Frank Sinatra used to hold his breath while swimming underwater.

Exercise 4

Here's a vocal exercise to improve your resonance.

Take a breath, then say each of these vowel sounds while pushing the air from the diaphragm, (the muscle below your lungs).

- ay
- ee
- ah
- oh
- oo

This exercise makes your voice strong and sure. To avoid your voice trailing off in places, remember to deep breathe when you are on the phone.

7. Pauses

If there's silence after you ask a question, stay comfortable with the pause. Your prospect is probably thinking.

And if you've asked a closing question (a question to which the answer suggests they are going ahead with an order) then silence is a good thing. Don't break it. Let them think it through uninterrupted.

Action

Here are eight ways to improve your tone of voice:

1. **Record** your voice and visualise the vocal range, the rise and fall. It is a boringly flat monotone? Or does it have energy and vocal variety?

2. **Listen** to radio announcers. Visualise the rise and fall of their voice as a line graph and notice their wide vocal range.

3. **Smile** when you answer the phone, because a smile can be heard through the phone.

4. As a way to gain rapport, remember to **match** your speed and volume to whoever you are talking. Practice varying speed, tone, inflection and volume for vocal variety.

5. **Gesture**. Wear a headset so your hands are free to gesture, which animates the voice. Or sometimes stand up when on the phone.

6. While on the phone, take frequent sips of **water**. It lubricates your throat and avoids sounding croaky.

7. Display **positive statements** at your workstation, such as:
   - I enjoy talking to new people.
   - I represent a great company and a great line of products.

8. Write out the **big picture benefit** of your product or service.

HOW TO CRAFT A CONVINCING RETURN ON INVESTMENT

Have you ever had a sales prospect tell you, *'I now have to convince my manager'* (or boss or head office, or whoever). As a buyer, do you ever have to convince another stakeholder?

When multiple decision-makers are involved, do you know how to calculate an accurate and plausible Return On Investment (ROI) for a product or service?

More sales are lost, not to a competitor, but to doing nothing. One way to move a decision forward is to include an ROI statement in your proposal.

But Business Case templates can be complex and highly structured. What's an example of a sales technique with a simple and quick cost/benefit statement that's easy to calculate and easy to understand?

Scenario 1
Library IT Upgrade

If calculating the benefit of upgrading a library's IT services you might focus on a measurable business problem effecting productivity; time spent by librarians looking for user IDs.

To illustrate how much time is being lost by librarians, (when they could be performing other more useful tasks), you might write:

THE BUSINESS CASE

— If 100 librarians each waste 10 minutes per day looking for user IDs
— that's 16.6 hours of time lost per day
    x $37 per hour estimated hourly rate
    = $616 cost per day

— annual lost revenue: $616 per workday
    x 235 workdays in a year
    = $144,760 value of lost time per annum

If improved user ID process saves 50% of time, that's a saving of $72,380.

ROI (RETURN ON INVESTMENT) FORMULA:
Gain minus Cost divided by Cost
(Gain − Cost) ÷ Cost

If to implement an improved process is $20,000, then:

ROI formula:

$$\frac{\text{Gain} - \text{Cost}}{\text{Cost}} \quad \text{or} \quad \frac{\$72,380 - \$20,000}{\$20,000}$$

ROI = 2.61 times or 261%

SUMMARY: For a once-off investment of $20,000 (plus your implementation costs), you can expect to achieve a minimum annual Return on Investment of 261% which will effectively have paid for itself within 6 months.

Scenario 2:
Presentation Skills Training

If calculating the benefit of Presentation Skills training for sales representatives, you can draw attention to the value of extra sales due to improved confidence, authority and influence. You might write:

THE BUSINESS CASE

What is one extra sale per person worth in a year?

If, as a result of this training, 10 representatives present with more confidence, more authority and more influence to gain even one extra client each in the next 12 months, with average sale worth $24,000*, then return in one year is potentially $240,000.

*My average sale might be a bit high, or low, but whatever calculation you use should produce a significant result.

ROI (RETURN ON INVESTMENT) FORMULA:
Gain minus Cost divided by Cost
(Gain – Cost) ÷ Cost

If cost of training for two days is $12,000
plus 10 salaries for two days
(estimate $11,550), then:

ROI formula:

$$\frac{\text{Gain} - \text{Cost}}{\text{Cost}} \quad \text{or} \quad \frac{\$240,000 - \$23,550}{\$23,550}$$

ROI = 9.19 times or 919%

SUMMARY: For a once-off investment of $23,550, you can expect to achieve a minimum annual Return on Investment of 919% which will effectively have paid for itself within a couple of months.

If you then add a statement about *the risk of doing nothing,* you have just created a compelling business case for your prospect to make a decision.

What Is Soft ROI?

As well as hard ROI expressed as dollars, there's soft ROI — emotional benefits, such as:

- reduced stress and frustration
- improved customer service
- faster response
- improved morale.

SOCIAL PROOF AS A WAY TO NEGOTIATE

Can you think of a time when a client considered your product or service too expensive or not right or just had any reason not to proceed?

Here's a classic negotiation tactic that can influence your client to change their mind, yet still 'save face'. Imagine your customer says, 'We would like to go ahead and buy (your product or service), but it's more than our budget allows.'

Using the Feel-Felt-Found approach you might say:

1. 'I can understand how you might **feel** that way.
2. 'Many of our clients **felt** initially it was more than they wanted to spend.
3. But after they went ahead, they **found** it actually saved money on training, overtime, and shrinkage.'

Here's Another Scenario

A not-for-profit organisation seeks a regular monthly donation. They ask, 'Would you consider making a regular monthly gift of $50 per month?' The possible new donor replies, 'Although I support what you do, I can't afford $50 a month.'

Using feel-felt-found, the fundraiser replies,

1. 'I can understand how you might **feel** that way.
2. 'Many of our regular donors **felt** that way at first.
3. 'But they decided to give it a go anyway, on the understanding they can cancel their donation any time. And do you know what? They **found** over time, there always was enough money to continue their pledge.'

(Then ask a question. Pause for the answer.)

4. 'On the understanding you can cancel anytime, would you be willing to give it a go?'

Feel-Felt-Found Works More Often Than It Doesn't

There is a human need to belong, to heed the crowd. It's what Robert Cialdini calls, in his book, *Influence: The Psychology Of Persuasion*[6], social proof. People do things they see other people doing.

Do you enter an empty restaurant, or one that is full of patrons? If you see a crowd gathered, does curiosity compel you to find out what the fuss is about? To test this out, try looking up into the sky in a public place. Notice how many others will then look up into the sky to see what you are seeing. It's a basic instinct.

A tip: Be careful how you say it. Don't say, *I **know** how you feel.'* This choice of words sometimes produces an angry response. You can't ever really know how another person feels. Say instead, *I **can understand** how you might feel that way.'* or, *I can imagine how you must feel.'*

Another Scenario

A customer is concerned if they purchase new technology it will be too complex and take too much time for team members to master. They might object with, *I think it's hard to understand and will take too long to get up to speed.'* Using feel-felt-found, you might respond with:

1. 'I can understand how you might **feel** that way, < name >.
2. 'Many of our clients **felt** the same way . . .
3. '. . . until they started using the platform and **found** it quicker to master than they at first thought.'

What are typical objections with your product or service that could be successfully handled with the 'Feel-felt-found' approach?

e.g. Objection, 'It's too . . . '

Now respond with,

Feel: 'I can understand why you'd **feel** that way . . .
Felt: 'Many of our clients **felt** . . .
Found: 'But what they **found** was . . .

Having a structured verbal template helps you think on your feet and sound confident when a prospect gives you a reason not to take the next step.

Sharpen your office etiquette

HOW TO REMEMBER PEOPLE'S NAMES AND NEVER BE EMBARRASSED AGAIN

We don't hear the 'E' word' often these days; 'e' for etiquette. Yet courtesy and consideration are the glue of team relationships. When we display ongoing respect and regard for our colleagues, we cultivate a happier atmosphere where people thrive and do their best work.

Remembering people's names, particularly in business, is unquestionably a tremendous asset. Yet how many of us struggle to recall someone's name five seconds after we've met them, let alone weeks later when we run into them again?

Quite a few of us, if Macquarie Dictionary is anything to go by. It lists 'What's-his-name', 'Whatsit', 'Whatchamecallit' and 'Thingummyjig' as words with definitions.

From the age of 19 when I started in corporate training, I learned to commit many new names to memory each week. Sometimes I would start six new classes with 30 people in each. At the beginning of each course I was expected to perform a memory demonstration recalling each person's name. You might think I am simply gifted with capacity to remember. But this is not the case. Name recall is a skill anyone can acquire if they have desire to do so.

As someone who applies practical techniques for good memory, I am surprised and a bit disheartened when I hear people competing in their claims to worst memory . . . 'I have a terrible memory' or, 'You think you have a lousy memory? My memory's so bad, my wife has to introduce herself to me at breakfast'.

This kind of negative self-talk convinces the subconscious and becomes a self-fulfilling prophecy.

If you're one of many people who believe — for that's all it is, an erroneous belief — you have trouble remembering people's names, take heart. There is a way to remedy this social handicap and the first step involves belief.

Here are six steps to help you remember names at your next business or social gathering when you are introduced to a small group.

1. *Believe It's Possible*

Act as if you have a good memory. The feeling of certainty breeds confidence and subsequent actions to support that belief. When you feel confident in your memory, you proactively focus to capture information for later retrieval. You actually try instead of giving up before you've started.

2. *Change Your Self-Talk*

How often do people interrupt an introduction with a light-hearted, 'Oh, I'll never remember everyone's name.' Sound familiar?

Replace stating, 'I can't remember', with 'It will come to me later'.

Tell yourself, 'I have a good memory'. After a short time of reprogramming your sub-conscious, you may be surprised and delighted to find information and people's names at your fingertips!

3. *Focus*

Most people are passive (or lazy) at the moment of introduction and allow new names to fall away. You have to capture information before you can retrieve it from memory.

Make a conscious decision to remember, then next time the opportunity arises, focus, listen actively and be confident of your recall. Short-term or working memory improves significantly with practice.

4. *Rehearse And Reinforce*

When introductions are complete, don't be the first person to talk. Stand back and mentally review who you've met and their names. By testing your memory within 30 seconds, you indelibly etch their names in your consciousness. It has to do with creating brain cell connections which improves the chance of subsequent recall. Another possibility is to visualise the name on their forehead. (This works well for the 35% of the population who have a predominantly visual learning style.) Take it further: visualise the letters of their name in a bright colour like hot pink.

5. *Repeat Names In Conversation*

Use people's names straight away. You might say, 'Hi, David, nice to meet you', or 'Tell me David, who do you know at this party / meeting?' You could remark on their appearance, 'David, where did you get that great jacket?'

6. *Be The Host*

When the next new person joins your group, dazzle them by introducing this new person to others in the group. You may find your peers commenting, 'You have a phenomenal memory' (which becomes a self-fulfilling prophecy).

Brain muscle is like any other muscle. It grows stronger with exercise and eventually works automatically.

I'll give you an example from my life. Most of the time I use the techniques just described. But occasionally I forget, or the introduction happens too quickly, or I'm distracted.

At a party recently I was introduced to a woman. We didn't have a conversation. I didn't use her name and didn't even decide to remember. One week later swimming in the sea, a wet head bobbed up beside me. I couldn't even see her body and she looked quite different with wet hair. Yet from somewhere in my well-oiled memory, out popped her name, 'Hello, Val,' I said, surprising even myself. She hardly remembered me.

I encourage you to work out your memory. You'll be amazed at how effective it becomes. Then, at those serendipitous moments when you unexpectedly bump into people you've previously met, you'll make an impact and gain rapport by remembering their names.

GREAT OFFICE ETIQUETTE HELPS TEAMS THRIVE

I'm often asked what is the number one office blunder when it comes to team etiquette.

Covert Workplace Bullying

Let's face it. Demeaning, belittling or de-energising comments or behaviour not only creates friction; it's a form of workplace bullying, which goes beyond etiquette.

For example, I was delivering a workshop on Business Communication where one participant complained about someone blurting out in frustration at a meeting, 'I'm surrounded . . . !' (' . . . by idiots' is the unspoken half of that sentence.) There's no place for sarcasm. An atmosphere of mutual respect helps people perform better, communicate better and enjoy being at work.

Having said that, let's now focus on the emotional intelligence of team etiquette.

1. *Greet People Upon Arrival And Leaving*

Make it a point to say hello to everyone in your work area upon arrival, and good-bye at the end of the day. It's civil, it's friendly, and it's common courtesy, which is the glue of team relationships.

For every one of our relationships, whether at home or at work, we have an 'emotional bank account'. Every time we interact with a smile, eye contact and friendliness, we 'make a deposit'. Every time we are impatient or abrupt, we 'make a withdrawal'.

Where there are deposits in the emotional bank account, there is high trust.

Negative workplace behaviours such as tantrums, put-downs, glaring, cold-shouldering or gossip overdraws our emotional bank account. Those behaviours cultivate resentment.

That doesn't mean never disagreeing. Constructive debates over ideas are the right kind of friction, which is healthy in teams.

2. *Email Etiquette*

All emails should pass the 'light of day' test. How would you feel if your angry or sarcastic email went viral on social media or was published on the front page of a newspaper?

This happened a few years back when a London lawyer insisted a secretary who spilt tomato sauce on his trousers pay his dry cleaning bill. He was compelled to resign after his email was published on the front page of *The Times* and widely circulated on the web.[3]

Remember the six-hour rule. If you write an email in anger, wait at least six hours, re-read and edit before sending.

The other rule is, 'Don't escalate over email'. If it requires a long-winded explanation, don't email. Know when to pick up the phone or speak face-to-face.

3. *Writing Emails*

The early days of stream of consciousness emails with no punctuation, no capitals, incorrect spelling, are gone. Email replaced the business letter. How you communicate in writing expresses your professionalism (or lack of).

A Royal Mail survey[4] in the UK indicated that 74% of customers distrust businesses using poor spelling or grammar, while 30% say they won't buy any product or service from them.

You need good grammar, spelling and punctuation. At the very least, use spell check to overview each email before it goes out.

4. *Personal Issues*

Our work team is our other family and it's ok to hope our colleagues will give us emotional support when we are going through a temporarily difficult time. So we shouldn't clam up about what's happening in our lives.

But beware of compassion fatigue. Your team mates' tolerance soon wears thin if the same issue is mentioned almost daily for weeks or even months on end. It can lose you respect.

There are distinct boundaries too. Any topic that makes people feel uncomfortable — sex, religion, politics, race — should be avoided. And know the difference between showing interest vs prying into people's personal affairs.

5. *Office Romance*

It's inevitable. People are working longer hours so more people are meeting their future spouse at work.

The problem is how to remain civil if you break up. It's important to keep it discreet but not secret, and to give some serious thought to the possibility of a break-up.

An office romance is when the two people involved are single. It's an office 'affair' if one or both parties are married — need I say, that should be avoided. It only causes heartache.

6. *Talking About Money*

Asking a colleague from the same organisation how much they earn is the biggest no-no at work! It's confidential and can create waves.

Asking someone what they paid for their house or their car or their jacket — is also considered rude.

On the other side of the coin, flaunting the cost of things is also awkward. If you are suffering financial difficulties, keep it to yourself. Those listening might feel pressure to offer a loan, which is inappropriate in the workplace.

If in a financial predicament, get help from an outside expert such as your accountant or financial advisor.

7. *Gossip*

Gossip is talking about other people, usually in their absence, and often in a disapproving tone. This is demeaning, belittling behaviour referred to earlier. The old adage applies here, if you can't say something nice, don't say anything at all.

8. *Punctuality*

Disrespect of other people's time is disrespect of other people. Aim to be five minutes early for an office meeting, and ten minutes early for an outside business appointment. It's a mark of respect, and wins points if you want to influence or persuade.

And if you are host for an event, you absolutely must be the first one there to set up and meet and greet.

9. Swearing

Never swear at work. TV viewers are warned ahead of time about coarse language in a program so they have choice whether to watch or not. We are obliged to be at work, we're not obliged to listen to profanity while we're there.

10. Professional Dress

Business is fast; first impressions count. In the blink of an eye, people form an impression and make judgements about you, Malcolm Gladwell explores this what is called 'thin slicing' in his book: *Blink*.[1]

How you speak and dress sends a message of your personality, character, status, refinement and success. Career professionals say you should dress for the promotion you want. Act as if you already have that role and dress for it.

Stains

Of 1000 people surveyed in Australia by Galaxy Research[2] , one in seven admit they are okay going to work with a stain on their clothing. But more than 60% of Australians form a negative opinion of someone wearing a stain in public. Over 30% judge stained clothing in the workplace as unprofessional.

Only bad breath is considered worse than a stain, while a stain is viewed worse than unironed garments or scraggly hair.

Love life might suffer too. 13% would not want to date someone wearing stained clothes.

Does it show a lack of pride in one's appearance? 50% of respondents believe it does.

Here's a story from one of my research assistants. It was the second day of university for a student in her first year. At lunch she spilt tomato sauce down the front of her black and white shirt. Realising the first week is when you make all your new friends, and with two more lectures that day, she felt she'd make a poor impression with a huge stain on her top. So, to buy a new shirt, she caught a bus to the shops, 15 minutes away. She confided, *'I didn't want to be known as the Tomato Sauce Girl.'*

11. Dining Etiquette

Here are 5 quick tips:

1. Break bread with your hands, don't cut it. (Remember the phrase 'break bread with me'?)
2. Know correct cutlery code to indicate 'still eating' (implements separated) and 'finished eating', (implements together, either handles towards you, or handles to the right).
3. Spoon soup away from you.
4. Use fork and spoon for pasta.
5. If you invite someone to lunch or dinner to discuss business, you are the host and should pay the bill! (If you mention up front that it's your treat it can put you both at ease.)

WHAT ARE 5 ANNOYING OPEN-PLAN OFFICE BEHAVIOURS?

While open-plan office design keeps everyone in the loop and cultivates a high performing team atmosphere, there is a downside to working without walls.

1. Loudness

Do you unconsciously talk louder when on a long distance call or mobile? Cultivate a soft voice when speaking on the phone and if it's a protracted personal call, step outside or into another room to maintain privacy. Most people don't want to know the details of your personal life.

Similarly, avoid using a speakerphone in a shared environment.

A loud mobile phone ringtone can jolt people in the middle of a task. Especially annoying is a phone ringing out while the owner has gone to lunch. Remember to put your mobile phone to silent or vibrate while in the office.

To sneeze, to yawn, to burp is only human, but if too resonant it's disturbing e.g., when a simple sneeze becomes 'ah-choo!' or a yawn becomes an emphatic sigh and stretch, or a burp becomes a resounding belch. Minimise the sound of sneezes, yawns and burps as much as you can. And automatically say, 'Excuse me' after.

From a hygiene perspective, show consideration for the health of your workmates, especially in flu season, and always have a box of tissues handy to sneeze or cough into.

2. *Interrupting*

If a colleague is on the phone, don't hover waiting to pounce as soon as the phone call finishes. Everyone's entitled to their privacy when on a call.

Be aware if body language indicates they are deep in concentration. Research shows it can take up to six minutes for a worker to resume after the briefest of interruptions, so resist the temptation to interrupt to ask a quick question.

Most people do leave their desk periodically, so why not save your questions until they are up and around.

3. *Eavesdropping*

Have you ever had a phone conversation, then subsequently the person in the next cubicle offered their opinion or answered a question they overheard? This can create an uncomfortable feeling of constantly being scrutinised.

'Prairie dogging' can be just as bad. Don't suddenly pop your head over the divider to see what's going on next door. It can be perceived as an invasion of privacy.

4. Swearing At The Computer

A harmonious workplace is filled with harmonious people. Becoming angry or frustrated with events, people or equipment makes everyone want to duck for cover. And there's never an excuse for bad language.

5. Odours

Just as too much perfume can be overwhelming, no one enjoys being near bad breath or body odour.

Daily flossing between your teeth and brushing your tongue aids in fresh breath. Yes, take a daily shower and yes, use a deodorant. If your deodorant causes skin irritation, try one that is not also an antiperspirant or does not contain aluminium. Health food stores sell alternative deodorants that work.

Stinky food smells from eating at your desk can irritate others, for example, microwaved tuna and cheese melt, fish curry, onions or garlic.

Why not, instead of eating lunch 'al desko' (at your desk), go for a short break, stretch your legs and refresh your brain. You'll most likely discover you are more productive for the rest of the afternoon.

INTRODUCTIONS — HOW TO PROPERLY INTRODUCE A VIP

I am often asked what is the etiquette of introductions; who is introduced to whom?

There is one simple rule to remember. Always start by saying first the name of the most important person. After that, everyone else is introduced to that person.

But who is considered 'the most important'? In business, it's not age or gender, but rank or status.

For example, a visitor to your workplace is the most important. Introduce anyone from your organisation to the visitor by saying the visitor's name first. Similarly, introduce a junior manager to a senior manager by saying the senior manager's name first.

What To Say?

Simply use the phrase *'this is'*. This construction keeps you to the format:

< Important person's name >, *this is* < lesser authority person's name >.

This is correct.

Avoid Saying . . .

Avoid using the phrase 'to meet', e.g. 'Mary Smith, I would like you to meet Bob Jones.'

Although you've started with Mary Smith's name first (as the person of greater authority), the phrase *'I would like you to meet'* turns it around, so Bob Jones now sounds like the more important person.

So avoid the danger of the phrase *'to meet'* in your introduction. Similarly, avoid including *'you to'* or *'to you'*, as it can place emphasis on the wrong person. Notice the difference in emphasis between:

Mary Smith, may I introduce **you to** Bob Jones.

vs

Mary Smith, may I introduce **to you** Bob Jones.

So leave 'to you' or 'you to' out of your wording altogether.

Responding

A simple *'Hello Mary'* or *'How are you, Bob?'* are fine. *'How do you do'* is appropriate in formal situations. And repeating their name is an aid to memory and cultivates rapport.

Groups

When one person joins a group, first introduce the individual to the group, then the group to the individual.

For example, 'Mary Smith, this is Bob Jones, Kym Voon, Seth Goldberg and Terry Seeto. Everyone, this is Mary Smith.'

Final Points

- Stand up when meeting people. It shows respect.
- Smile and use good eye contact.
- Use both first and last names.
- As an icebreaker, to help start the conversation, add some information about the person e.g. their job title or organisation.

Action

1. When you are about to introduce people, remember to ask yourself, 'Who is the person of greater authority?'.
2. Then use the greater authority name first, followed by, '... *this is*...'
3. Add extra information about job role to assist conversation to flow.
4. As an aid to memory, repeat their name in conversation.

IMPRESS PEOPLE BY FINE-TUNING YOUR HANDSHAKE

Handshakes, like most social rituals, are a delicate art form. While a good one can warm hearts and open doors, a poor handshake can make a recipient feel uncomfortable, perturbed or just plain irritated.

Apart from the embarrassment of forgetting someone's name, nothing feels worse than a handshake gone horribly wrong.

A 'just right' shake is firm, web-to-web, (the web being the skin between the thumb and the index finger), and coming in at the right angle, with your hand vertical.

Some people judge you by the quality of your handshake, so it makes sense to perfect it.

How Many Pumps?

One definite pump is fine. Some people like one-and-a-half pumps. But stretch that to two or three and it starts to feel like too much. It's as if you're trying too hard. However be mindful of cultural differences. In some European countries multiple pumps is the norm.

Pressure

Remember the 'Goldilocks principle': not too strong, not too weak, but just right!

Once I was on the receiving end of a 'bone crusher'. My ring was being ground into my hand and I literally buckled at the knees with pain. Although I flinched, I acted as if nothing had happened.

On the other hand, a limp-handed flutter is not good either. Make it firm and definite.

Grip

As well as avoiding the 'bone-crusher' and the 'limp fish', steer clear of strange grips. I had someone grab me by my fingertips and not pump but more 'vibrate' my hand. I've experienced people come in with their wrist bent sideways. It felt awkward and left a golf-ball sized gap between our palms.

Other handshake variations to avoid include the aggressive 'rotator', where the recipient's hand is gripped and turned downwards in an overt power play. Rotating your colleague's hand goes beyond confident to dominating. It sends a negative message.

Former Australian Prime Minister, John Howard was photographed doing a 'rotator' on the then leader of the opposition, Mark Latham. Latham responded with an equally bad 'pull-in', where the shaker's hand hauls the person towards them.[5]

Finally, double-handed shakes, although regularly performed by politicians, are unacceptable unless exchanged between long-time friends.

Gender And Cultural Diversity

Once upon a time in Western culture, it was polite for men to wait for women to first offer their hand. These days, the rules around handshakes and gender are more relaxed and it doesn't matter whether a man or woman offers their hand first.

Both men and women should be aware though, that in some regions of the world it's the norm for a man to avoid shaking the hand of a woman. Be sensitive to cultural differences, especially when travelling overseas.

Ask Your Friends To Rate Your Handshake

What you don't know about your handshake can harm your career. Practice with your friends. Ask them to rate your grip, pump and pressure and be prepared to adjust according to their feedback.

Remember, your handshake says a lot about you and should be regarded as part of an overall business communication strategy.

HOW TO STAND OUT WITH A SIMPLE THANK-YOU CARD

How you say thank you can be a competitive advantage! Because the handwritten thank-you note is so rare these days, writing one helps you stand out.

A Lenox (US giftware company) etiquette poll[6] discovered that almost 50% of people forget to say 'thank you'.

Success in business, as in life, is all about the details. Writing a personalised note of thanks communicates that you value and respect someone's time and contribution. It forges relationships, which can turn into opportunities.

When people feel valued and respected, they are more responsive. The next time you ask them to do something beyond their usual job description they remember your past appreciation and professionalism.

I am sometimes asked, 'But won't a follow-up email or phone call do?' The quick answer is, it might 'do', but it doesn't 'differentiate'. An email or phone call is expected. A card sent in the mail exceeds expectations.

When to Send A Handwritten Thank-You Card

Many occasions demand a written thank-you:

- you have a guest at a special dinner or lunch
- a thank-you for a gift
- a personal milestone in a colleague's life (birth, death, promotion . . .)
- any time someone has gone out of their way to assist you.

What To Say

It's ok to keep a thank-you card simple and brief; three sentences are all it takes.

1. Refer to the event and how much you appreciated it. (Don't use the words 'thank you' yet. Wait for the second sentence.)
2. Acknowledge something specific and thank them for that.
3. Refer to a future meeting or contact, or their future success.

Case Study:

There's a story about a staff member who, after visiting the interstate office for three days, sent handwritten thank-you notes to everyone who spent significant time with him.

Dear Jim

The opportunity to learn your systems and how you make things happen in your office is truly appreciated.

Thanks for your suggestions about how we can make changes in our division; I am inspired by your ideas.

I look forward to catching up with you again at the Melbourne meeting.

All the best

Michael Conrad

A week later, the writer of the cards received a call from the manager of that office saying, 'Everyone here is talking about your cards. It was completely unnecessary, and entirely appreciated. It's no wonder people love dealing with you. If there's ever anything I can do for you, let me know, and please feel free to come back any time.'

Action

1. Keep some high quality thank-you cards (or blank cards) and postage stamps on hand. Then it only takes one minute to write your three sentences, stamp and address your envelope and post.
2. Take advantage of online services where you can personalise the wording and add your own photos. They'll even send it out in the mail for you at a cost-effective rate.

Gather
wisdom

READ YOUR WAY TO THE TOP

What makes some people successful and others not? One answer is that most successful people are voracious readers. Their curiosity is intact.

Warren Buffet
One of the wealthiest individuals in the world, CEO of Berkshire Hathaway and billionaire investor, Warren Buffet, spends 80% of his working day reading and thinking. Pointing to a stack of books, Buffet said, 'Read 500 pages like this every day. That's how knowledge works. It builds up, like compound interest. All of you can do it, but I guarantee not many of you *will* do it.'[12]

Steve Siebold
Over the last 30 years author Steve Siebold interviewed 1200 of the richest people. In his book, *How Rich People Think*,[13] he writes, 'Walk into a wealthy person's home, and one of the first things you'll see is an extensive library of books they've used to educate themselves on how to become more successful.'

Elon Musk
Entrepreneur, inventor and engineer, Elon Musk's curiosity is voracious. 'I was raised by books,' says Musk.[14] 'You don't know what you don't know. You realize there are all these things out there,' says Musk.[15] According to his mother, Maye, at age nine he read the entire Encyclopedia Britannica, 'and remembered it'.[16]

Oprah Winfrey
Oprah Winfrey is credited with saying, 'Books were my pass to personal freedom. I learned to read at age three, and soon discovered there was a whole world to conquer that went beyond our farm in Mississippi.' Bill Gates says he reads 50 books a year. 'This is one of the things I love about reading,' Gates said. 'Each book opens up new avenues of knowledge to explore.'[17]

Dame Anita Roddick
At age ten, Dame Anita Roddick read a book about the Holocaust which awakened her sense of natural justice.[18]

The list of billionaire entrepreneurs and successful people who are avid readers is long and includes Mark Zuckerberg, Ellen DeGeneres, Anthony Robbins, Mark Cuban . . . and a whole lot more.

Gather Wisdom 10 Minutes A Day

Did you know that 50% of books sold are never read? Amazing, isn't it? That's like paying money to a health club then never showing up.

The average person reads 250 words per minute. A typical paperback has around 350 words per page. By reading ten minutes a day, you'll get through seven pages a day. This means you can read a typical length book of around 150 pages in 21 days.

Even with longer books, if you read ten minutes a day you'll be able to finish a book a month. By the end of a year, you'll have read at least 12 books; by the end of 10 years, it adds up to more than 120 books.

Consider . . . by setting aside just ten minutes a day, you can easily read 120 books that can help you grow richer in knowledge and wisdom in all areas of your life. Where else can you get that kind of return in less time than it takes to do the dishes? People might say they don't have time to read, but that's just an excuse. They're using their time to do other things they value more than reading.

Find excuses *to* read. Ten minutes reading a day gives you a slight edge that reaps big dividends in your life. Reading ten minutes a day makes itself felt at the end of the year.

Action

1. Go to your bookshelf and find one of those books you bought a while ago but haven't started reading yet . . . then read it for ten minutes.
2. When you've done that, reflect; pause for another minute and think about what you've learnt. How much richer are you for having read that?
3. Learn how to double or triple your reading rate.[19] Improve the way your eyes access information via text.

Benefits of Voracious Reading

The French call it 'soif'; thirst for learning. Here are just some of the benefits of being an avid reader:

- keep up to date
- make better-informed decisions
- improve critical thinking, vocabulary and writing skills
- increase general knowledge, become a better conversationalist
- improve confidence and self-esteem
- avoid lag, become an early adopter, gain a competitive advantage, stay ahead of the curve
- discover that one good idea that will increase your income and net worth.

ARE WE IN DANGER OF LOSING OUR DEEP READING BRAIN?

If I asked you, 'Did you read a book in the last year?', could you say yes? 26% of Americans surveyed did not say yes.[1] That's the percentage who admitted they did not read a book within a 12-month period.

Is there a virtual book-burning going on? Bookshops are going out of business. Publishers are dying. Are people not reading books anymore?

As a speed reading instructor, I've observed how reading has changed over decades. Reading has become referencing. We click on hyperlinks, move sideways through multiple articles, moving from idea to idea rather than following deeply a single extended argument.

So my question is . . . are we in danger of losing our deep reading brain? Are we living in a post-literate society?

Literacy Shapes Thinking

Research was done with a tribe that did not read or write; they had only an oral tradition. They were given a puzzle to solve.[2]

In the far north where there is snow, all bears are white.

The place, Novaya Zemla, is in the far north.

What colour are the bears from Novaya Zemla?

A typical answer from someone from a pre-literate tribe runs along the lines of, 'I don't know. I've seen a black bear. I've never seen any other bears. Each locality has its own animals.'

While these people are no less intelligent, they do think differently.

They could not solve a problem of logic. Their thinking is more situational, based on experiences.

Ideas written down free you from a subjective approach. The more you read the more you understand that things are complex, not simple. And you can better tolerate ambivalence, that is, more than one viewpoint. You can avoid knee-jerk reactions to things. It helps to sharpen our minds. It's brain training.

Neuroplasticity

The scientific principle of neuroplasticity describes how the brain changes its structure and function in response to activity and mental experience.

Just as rats raised in a stimulated environment grow new brain cell connections, reading a book with an extended argument has the capacity to grow your ability for critical thinking and analysis.

It's important to read broadly. Just as people who don't exercise can't do certain things with their bodies, so, people who don't read can't do certain things with their minds.

What Happens If We Don't Read?

We're not opening our minds to other ways of looking at things. We devolve into seeing things as black and white; this is oversimplification. For example, George Orwell's novel, *Animal Farm*,[3] has characters, the Sheep, who repeat the slogan, 'Four legs good, two legs bad.' They simplified things down to its ridiculous essence.

So what can we do about it? Here are five ways.

Action

1. Don't feel pressured to read for long periods. Read for just ten minutes first thing in the morning or last thing at night. Reading is an exercise in mindfulness.

2. Some schools schedule DEAR events, drop-everything-and-read, for ten minutes. But is it happening in the workplace? Why not have a Drop-Everything-And-Read Friday? Just for ten minutes.

3. Read book summaries. A book summary is a good entrée into a book. It can capture your attention and make you want to read the entire book. (Incidentally, book summary websites often have a really great list of titles to read.)

4. Learn to speed read so you read more at the speed of thought.

5. Instead of just reading articles, blogs and posts, read whole books. They go deep and have capacity to transform our thinking.

Use it or lose it. Use your Deep Reading brain or lose it!

WHAT HABITS MAKE YOU A SLUGGISH READER?

Did you know ancient readers read aloud? Ancient writing was continuous sentences called Scriptio Continua[4] which lacked punctuation, upper or lower case, or word separation. Reading was aloud, mostly as a group activity.

One of the earliest recorded silent readers was St Ambrose, Bishop of Milan, from 374 AD. St Augustine wrote his observation that Ambrose, 'When he read, his eyes scanned the page and his heart sought out the meaning, but his voice was silent and his tongue was still.'[5] St Jerome, another learned monk from the fourth century, was also a silent reader.

In the West, it wasn't until the early Middle Ages, beginning in the seventh century, when the separation of words began[6] that reading transformed from group readings out loud to a silent, private activity. With Gutenberg inventing the printing press around 1439, books became easier to own and literacy more widespread.

But Is Reading Truly Silent?

The modern average reader sub-vocalises as they read; they silently listen to the sound of the words while reading. And it's sub-vocalisation that limits your reading rate. You are trapped into a reading speed no greater than the rate at which you can hear and process spoken word. Almost everyone sub-vocalises, or hears an inner reading voice. It is a carry-over from when we first learned to read by sounding out words and reading aloud.

(And no, we don't need to say the words to understand the words. Your brain is capable of direct eye to mind transfer of meaning.)

If you consult *Guinness Book of World Records*[7] you'll find the fastest talker was clocked at 655 words per minute (wpm) in 1995. Speed readers still sub-vocalise, but they minimise its impact. Only some of the words are heard mentally as they read. This enables them to read and comprehend above 1,000 wpm.

How Do You Minimise Sub-Vocalisation?

Simple answer . . . by reading too fast to hear all the words! With the right techniques, it is as simple as it sounds. Can you read the following sentence?

Eye sea two feat in our rheum.

If you heard this sentence spoken aloud rather than reading it, you might experience less difficulty to make out meaning. The sounds make sense but the spellings do not.

This demonstrates how the meaning of the written word does not come from sound of the words but from the spelling or the 'look' of the word. Words are recognised on sight, therefore we do not have to sub-vocalise to understand the meaning.

Do We Read With Our Eyes Or Our Brain?

When we scan a landscape, our eyes cannot move smoothly. They jerk and jump along spasmodically. No amount of mind-over-matter training will change the fact that unless the eyes are fixed on an object in motion they are tracking — a bird, a car, a moving finger — the eyes will not move continuously.

When looking around a room, your eyes move from one point of focus to another and perceive different visual information at each resting-point.

Your brain constructs a stable and coherent image of the room in your mind, despite your eyes constantly moving from point to point. While your retina is registering changing fragments of a room one at a time, your brain perceives the room as one integrated, perceptual whole.

Lack Of Eye-Movement Fluency

Have you ever watched someone's eyes as they're reading? If you observe someone reading, you'll notice a stop and start motion while they read. That problem is called lack of fluency.

It's like a learner driver whose car kangaroo hops down the road; rather than a skilled driver who drives in one smooth direction. Lack of fluency slows down your reading rate.

The technical term for this jerky motion is 'saccade' (from a French word meaning 'jerk'). So when the average reader reads they experience a jerky, saccadic eye movement.

Here's a simple demonstration. Close one eye and gently touch its eyelid by placing the base of your hand on your chin then let your fingertips lightly rest over the eyelid. With your other eye, slowly trace a line from left to right.

Can you feel jerking movements of the closed eye as it moves in synch with your other one?

Spot The Blooper

Next time you are watching a film or video and the scene calls for the actor to gaze at a moving object, observe . . . do the eyes follow smoothly or do they jerk along? If eye movement is smooth and stable, the actor had a moving object for their eyes to track. If eye movement is spasmodic, then the director committed a film-making blooper!

Regression

Another problem with eye movement is regression. Regression is where the eye flits back and rereads part of a word. It's almost imperceptible; most people don't even know they're doing it; you can't see it with the naked eye.

Eye movement cameras can measure the number of regressions the reader makes per page. They teach this in optometry school.

Did you know the average reader regresses around 50 or 60 times per page? And it slows down reading rate. Imagine driving down a suburban street, continuously stopping at each intersection, backing up a car-length before moving on. It's a time-waster.

Fixation

How many words do you *see* at one time while you read? Probably only one word at a time, the one you're reading? A problem of the average reader is they see only one word at a time, perhaps two or three, with a narrow focus. That's called fixation.

Speed readers can read whole lines at a time; that's around ten words at a time. In fact, there's a Chinese saying referencing speed reading, 'one eye, ten lines' or ☒ ☒ ☒ ☒ .[8]

Learning to speed read shifts you from reading individual words to reading ideas. That's where you save time as well.

Summary

You can increase your reading speed significantly by learning techniques to overcome the poor reading habits of:

- sub-vocalisation
- lack of eye-movement fluency
- regression
- fixation

If you spend 30% of your time at work or study reading and you double your reading rate, you've just freed up an additional 15% of time for other things — or you can read more in the same amount of time.

COLLAPSE TIME AND REDUCE INFORMATION OVERLOAD

Do you read everything at about the same rate, or do you have faster rates when reading for overview and slower rates reading for detail?

Can you vary your reading rate depending on:

- difficulty of the material
- your familiarity with the subject
- your purpose for reading it?

Mature readers break the habit of reading everything at one constant rate and have cultivated the capacity to adjust their speed to the material.

Suppose you plan to take a 240-kilometre car journey. You might encounter hills, curves and a mountain pass, as well as straight and level sections.

The total journey might take three hours, averaging 80 kph. While driving, you may slow down to 40 kph on curves and hills, then on straight, level sections you could travel up to 100 kph. Similarly, avoid using a single speed when reading. It's too rigid.

Read easy, familiar material more swiftly. To gain an overview, scan through detailed explanations that are not so relevant to your purpose. That way you can pick up the gist or working knowledge of a text or locate specific information.

Read more slowly long, wordy sentences (so you can untangle the ideas). To understand unfamiliar, abstract information or detailed, technical material, also read slower.

Take shortcuts. It's ok to skip material not necessary for your purpose. Good readers are flexible readers. They know how and when to shift gears when reading and use several different speeds.

They use low gear when the going is steep, and shift into high gear in the straight sections. You can too.

Action

1. Read with a flexible reading rate: accelerate and decelerate.
2. Use the Macroreading® previewing technique described in the next chapter.
3. Attend a speed reading workshop or enrol in an online program[9] and learn how to and double or triple your current reading rate without loss of comprehension.

SPEED READING HACK: DOUBLE YOUR READING RATE WITH MACROREADING®

Often the content of a non-fiction book is more important as a whole rather than all its details. If you have only an hour to spend on a book or document, it makes sense to scan all of it roughly in that hour than to read in detail only part of it from the beginning.

There is a way to scan reading material twice as fast as your comfortable reading rate that's effective and saves you time. It's called Macroreading®[10]. (It's not exactly skim reading, nor is it speed reading, but if you Macroread® on a daily basis, it may trigger your brain to get used to fast input and subsequently read faster.) This method is described in my book on how to study, *Brainpower Smart Study: How To Study Effectively Using a Tested and Proven 8-step Method.*[11]

Overview

Look first at the big picture by starting with an overview of your material. The goal is simply to gain a general idea of the content, the gist of it. Relax as you preview. You can't expect to fully understand it at this preview stage. You'll read for understanding later.

Aid To Memory

When it comes to remembering what we read, we recall more if we allow the mind to first register the information with a fast overview. Have you ever watched a movie a second time and noticed things that escaped your attention on first viewing? When the goal is to remember what you've read, previewing before reading for detail is beneficial.

Then during the read-for-understanding we recognise what previously registered during the preview. Multiple reading in this way aids memory.

Aid To Understanding

Previewing is not only an aid to memory, it's an aid to understanding. It is good practice to start wide, gain a global view first, then go deep, to focus on the detail.

Easy Way To Start

Do you ever find it difficult to open a book or report to even begin to read? A preview is less demanding and eases you effortlessly into action.

How Fast Is A Preview?

A comfortable preview rate varies from person to person. For most people, twice as fast as their comfortable read-for-understanding rate is about right.

An average reader reads around 200 — 300 words per minute. Their preview rate might be around 400 — 600 words per minute — twice as fast as their usual reading rate. If a typical paperback has around 300 words per page, then it might take around 30 seconds to preview a page.

For a speed reader who reads above 1000 words per minute (and that's with good understanding or it's not speed reading), their preview rate might be 2000 words per minute or around 11 seconds per page.

Macroreading ®

In our Speed Reading program we teach a method of previewing we call Macroreading ® which is scanning the text with a relaxed eye focus, at a rate around twice as fast as your comfortable reading rate, to gain an overview.

Macroreading® is more systematic and strategic than skim reading (which is simply picking out keywords).

Zigzag Or S

To Macroread®, tell your eyes to slightly defocus, then move your finger, hand or a pen as a visual aid in a zigzag or 's' motion down the page, scanning all the words twice as fast as a comfortable, read-for-understanding rate, to pick up the gist or general overview.

You can go through an entire book this way in less than an hour to grasp the overall structure and theme of the book. Then when you're ready to read for detail, you will know where to go, always in the context of the whole. And when you read, target only those specific areas of the text you want or need to know; allow yourself to read in order of usefulness and appeal. It's ok to skip sections that don't interest you.

Much unnecessary reading can be eliminated at this preview stage, thus saving time. (By the way, this method is reserved for non-fiction. It won't work for fiction with a linear storyline.)

What Is 'Proper' Reading Anyway?

In previewing, you are not reading for detail. Just allow your eyes to scan over the material, gaining a feel for the big picture, picking up the gist.

I don't agree with, 'If you don't read it properly you may as well not read it at all'. What is 'proper' reading anyway? You might ask yourself, 'Isn't it a waste of time scanning words this way? How is it possible to read and understand at twice as fast as my comfortable reading rate?'

Well, here's the secret: skilled readers don't read everything at the same rate. They match their reading rate to their purpose.

In my experience as a speed reading instructor, I've observed many CEOs and Senior Managers use their own method of scanning or skimming as a way to get through their 'must reads'. If all you need is an overview of a text, then previewing is proper reading.

Personally, I don't read everything at one single base rate. As a skilled reader, I use a range of reading rates. I match my rate to my purpose. I can choose to speed up and scan when all I want to extract is an overview. I can slow down to a comfortable pace to read for understanding.

Become a skilled reader; read with a variable reading rate depending on your purpose.

Action

1. Macroread® non-fiction for the big picture first.
2. Then read-for-detail in order of interest.
3. Exceed 19 books per year on success, attitude, peak performance.
4. Keep a reading log of what you read.

HOW TO MEASURE YOUR READING RATE

Have you ever been curious to know your reading rate? Before improving reading rate through the Macroreading ® technique described in the previous chapter, does it make sense to first measure your current reading speed, so you can compare again later? Here's an easy way to calculate your rate, using your own reading material.

What You Need

- reading material — paperback or hardback book in easy-to-read fiction or non-fiction
- countdown timer — (smartphone app ok)
- calculator
- two paperclips or sticky notes to mark start and end

Note: Reading onscreen can be up to 40% slower than reading on paper. That's why I suggest reading a physical book for this calculation.

Instructions

1. Mark beginning line with a paperclip, post-it or pencil tick. Set timer for 3 minutes.
2. Start timer and read for good understanding for 3 minutes.

3. When timer sounds, stop, mark end with a pencil tick, paperclip or sticky note.
4. Before calculating reading rate, you might like to self-test your comprehension and memory.

To check your recall, simply turn the reading material face down and verbalise a brief summary out loud to yourself for 30 seconds.

Rate your summary, whether it's:

- Excellent
- Very good
- Good
- Average
- Below par

Calculate Reading Rate

- Words per line. Count total words (containing two or more letters) on two lines then divide by two.
- Number of lines. Count number of lines you read in 3 minutes.

WORDS PER LINE x NUMBER OF LINES ÷ MINUTES = WORDS PER MINUTE

- Multiply words per line by number of lines read; then divide by 3 (minutes). This is your words per minute rate.

What's Average?

- 200-300 words per minute is a typical reading rate.
- 300-500 wpm is above average.
- 500-1000 wpm is a skilled reading rate.
- Exceeding 1000 wpm — if you self-rated your understanding and memory as excellent to very good, then congratulations, you are a speed-reader!

Stay curious

Following our curiosity breathes new life into us by taking us down a different path. Like the cat, it's like we have nine adventurous-amazing lives instead of one safe-average one.

CURIOSITY HAS NINE LIVES

You know what's scary about the saying, 'Curiosity killed the cat'? This proverb paints a negative picture of inquisitiveness; when being curious is the very stuff of innovation and creativity.

Curiosity Quotient (CQ)

Curiosity is different to intelligence. It's possible to have high IQ with a low curiosity quotient (CQ). An intellectually curious person, someone with high CQ, reads widely, not just in their own area of expertise, but from a wide range of subjects. They'll probably also pursue a variety of recreational activities and may master numerous leisure pursuits over the course of their life.

Why Be Curious?

Following our curiosity can lead us to bubble over with new ideas, creativity and innovation. Taking action around new ideas as they come up can add a sense of purpose and meaning to our life, making us more optimistic and confident about the future.

It's self-fulfilling. It's an antidote against feelings of stagnation and hopelessness.

Doing something new can make you happy. Feel stuck in a rut? To shift things, to get unstuck, consider your input. Doing something new inspires us, adds a sense of fun and pleasure and contributes to our overall level of happiness and wellbeing.

Being open to new experiences cultivates psychological flexibility. By becoming a person of many dimensions, life offers better choices. New doors will open.

Don't Follow Your Passion, Follow Your Curiosity

Common advice is to follow your passion. But what if you don't have a passion or you've lost it?

Author Elizabeth Gilbert describes[1] a time when, after the success of her book, *Eat, Pray, Love,* she faltered writing the draft of her next book. She realised she'd lost the spark to write. On the advice of a friend, she took a break from following her 'passion' of writing, backed off for a while, and followed her curiosity instead, 'with its humble, roundabout magic.' Gardening allowed her to think by not thinking. Months later while gardening, an idea of how to fix her book popped into her head. She was then able to restart her second book, *Committed*.

Einstein's Brain

Albert Einstein is acknowledged as an intellectual giant of the 20th century. How was his brain shape different?

After his death at age 76 in 1955, Einstein's brain was preserved and analysed. Weighing about 12% less than the average adult male brain, the cerebral cortex was also thinner. In areas of the cortex specialising in 3D perception and mathematical thought, Einstein's brain was unique. His parietal regions were larger and shaped differently to other human brains. In fact, his parietal regions were so large, each hemisphere was about 15% wider than other brains studied. There's even evidence of his early training in playing the violin.[2]

Does Brain Size Matter?

In Einstein's case the answer is, *not necessarily*. But could these differences in brain shape explain Einstein's insights into space and time?

Neuroplasticity

One of the great findings of brain research in late 20th century is that brain shape is not fixed, but malleable, like plastic. Brain shape can change, especially when influenced by an enriched environment or when regularly presented with new information and stimuli. Not only does what we think about change the brain, but neural plasticity means that doing something new stimulates your brain to grow new brain cell connections.

An early clue about plasticity was the observation that canary brains grow larger in the singing season.[3] A 1998 landmark study about the human brain showed it can develop new brain cells.[4]

This kicked off a whole raft of scientific studies connecting learning activity with brain changes. Because London taxi drivers are required to memorise 'the Knowledge', (central London's complex layout of 25,000 streets and thousands of places of interest), a study in 2000 revealed taxi drivers who successfully passed the training, experienced brain changes. Their hippocampus increased in size after the training, and memory improved. Professor Maguire who led the study remarked, 'The human brain remains plastic even in adult life, allowing it to adapt when we learn new tasks.'[5] This finding suggests there's hope not only for rehabilitation after brain injury but also benefits to the brain from lifelong learning.

German researchers asked subjects over three months to learn to juggle a three-ball cascade, sustaining it for at least one minute.[6] After three months, brain scans revealed that in response to daily juggling, certain areas of the brain had grown. Subjects were then instructed to stop juggling and again after three months fresh brain scans determined the increase in grey matter had reduced. This suggests with brain activity, it's use it or lose it; we should challenge the brain with learning new skills or information.

Similar studies have been done on brains of professional musicians, people who are bilingual, medical students before and after exams and Buddhist monks who meditated.

Build Self-Efficacy

When you attempt something new, you may be surprised to discover you can actually do it well. This boosts what psychologists call self-efficacy; confidence that if I can do this, it is likely I can do other things well too. It breeds optimism and a feeling of success.

Pick A New Activity and Master It

Peter Drucker (1909-2005), considered the top management thinker of his time, attempted a new and different hobby every three years. 'Every three or four years I pick a new subject,' he wrote. 'It may be statistics, it may be medieval history, it may be Japanese art, it may be economics. Three years of study are by no means enough to master a subject, but they are enough to understand it. So for more than sixty years, I have kept on studying one subject at a time.

'This has not only given me a substantial fund of knowledge. It has forced me to be open to new disciplines and new approaches and new methods — for every one of the subjects I have studied, makes different assumptions and employs a different methodology.'[7]

Is there a new skill you secretly yearn to master if you only had time or confidence to try?

Remind yourself that attempting something new turns the lights on in your brain, staves off senility and promotes mental flexibility.

How To Keep Your Genius Juices Flowing

Brain function doesn't have to decline with age; learning something new activates the brain, stimulates it, and keeps it young. Doctors encourage people to perform daily mental activity such as crosswords or sudoku as a way to stimulate the brain.

If you feel stuck, revive your spirit of curiosity. If you've lost your passion and energy, become more curious.

Don't Just Do What You're Good At

Challenge yourself by learning a skill you *don't* have a natural talent for. A friend of mine recognised he was poor at dancing. To fix this, he didn't just go along to a few dance classes. He enrolled for a Diploma qualification requiring regular class attendance, study, practice and exams. At his group's graduation performance, while not the absolute best dancer, his technique was equivalent to the majority of his peers. Daily practice transformed his kinetic inability.

Curiosity Opens Doors

Imagine you overhear in a cafe two science students discussing the impact of the LHC on the environment. Your curiosity is awakened to find out, what exactly is the LHC? A web search reveals they're referring to the Large Hadron Collider in Switzerland. Suddenly you find yourself reading about atom smashing, proton beams, luminosity, inverse femtobarns and neutrino masses.

Subsequently, when planning a trip to Europe, you find yourself booking a side-trip to Geneva to experience a guided tour of the LHC. This side-visit has the capacity to become more than a simple half-day leisure activity. Depending on who you meet and your response to the experience, doesn't it have the potential to change the trajectory of your life?

When Steve Jobs delivered the Commencement Address at Stanford University in 2005 he told a story about how, after dropping out of his formal course, he was attracted to study calligraphy. 'Much of what I stumbled into by following my curiosity and intuition turned out to be priceless later on,' Steve explained. 'If I had never dropped out, I would have never dropped in on this calligraphy class, and personal computers might not have the wonderful typography that they do.'[8]

Jobs learned a skill before he needed that skill. Sometimes life is understood in reverse. It was years after studying calligraphy that the benefit of that skill manifested in his design approach.

Invest in yourself. You are your own best asset. As you invest in yourself with courses, certifications, skills, the more valuable the asset — you — becomes.

You Are a Genius . . . At Something

A genius is someone who can put two dissimilar ideas together and come up with a fresh idea. 'Some of the most significant ideas come about when someone sees a problem in a new way — often by combining disparate elements that initially seemed unrelated,' writes Dorie Clark.[9]

A genius doesn't have to be good at everything; anyone can be a genius at something if they focus, research and invest time to reflect on a question, problem or issue.

Architect and inventor, Buckminster Fuller said, 'The things to do are: the things that need doing, that you see need to be done, and that no one else seems to see need to be done.'[10]

The Japanese philosophy of Kaizen suggests the real work we should be doing in the world is continuous improvement; constant reinvention. Look around, focus on a product or an action and ask yourself, 'How else can we do this?'. The next chapter, *Reinvent*, explores the philosophies of Kaizen, Marginal Gains and the 1% Improvement Rule.

Multiple Intelligences

Intelligence is more than being good at English or Maths. There are eight intelligences, and individuals display a different mix of the eight.[11]

1. *Linguistic-Verbal Intelligence*

   Like to read and write? Good at languages? That's being word smart.

2. *Logical-Mathematical Intelligence*

   Are you good at maths and solving problems? That's number smart.

3. *Interpersonal Intelligence*

   Enjoy socialising with others? Belong to a club? You are people smart.

4. *Intrapersonal Intelligence*

   Enjoy working on your own? Keep a personal diary? That's being self smart.

5. *Musical Intelligence*

   Can you remember songs? Play a musical instrument? You are music smart.

6. *Visuo-Spatial Intelligence*

   Good at art? Or packing the boot of a car? Able to put things together from a diagram, or read a map? Visual and spatial intelligence makes you picture smart.

7. *Bodily-Kinesthetic Intelligence*

   Are you good at swimming, athletics, gymnastics or dance? Good with your hands? That's body smart.

8. *Naturalist Intelligence*

   Enjoy being in nature? Can you name plants and animals? That's nature smart.

It's easy to go through life thinking some people are smart, some dumb. But consider instead how people can be intelligent in different ways. What if someone can build a motorcycle from spare parts but doesn't excel at written tests? Feel good about what you're good at and admire others for where their abilities lie.

For a garden to grow you have to water it, and it's the same for your brain. A lazy brain does the same thing day after day; whereas challenging the brain with new and different activities builds new neural pathways. To give your brain a workout, try swapping the hand you usually brush your teeth with or change the route you travel to work.

Stand Up. Sit Less. Move More

Regular exercise increases brain function by stimulating new cells to form in the hippocampus — the part of the brain crucial for memory and learning.[12] In my Time Management presentations, when I ask the audience if they take a lunch break away from their desk, I'm disappointed to discover a trend for people to eat lunch at their desk while continuing to work.

In scans of the brain after sitting quietly for 20 minutes contrasted with just after a walk,[13] brain activity is greater after physical movement. This leads to better cognition, faster, better decisions, more accurate responses.

Here's the lesson. At work find reasons to frequently take a micro-break to get up from your desk. Here's a list of tactics:

- have lunch away from your desk
- take a fresh air break
- walk over to talk in person instead of sending an email
- drink more water so you refill the glass (or go to the bathroom) more often
- use a bathroom that's further away
- park your car further away
- locate your wastepaper bins further away so you have to rise from your desk
- use stairs instead of the lift
- walk around the block at lunch
- use a stand-up desk
- introduce stand-up meetings
- use a headset and stand during phone calls
- aim to reduce sitting by two hours per day

8 Ways to Reboot Your Brain

It's never too late to defrag our mind, reboot our brain, refresh our creativity and find pleasure in finding things out. Here are 8 ways. But the list is endless.

1. Do something new.

Find a public event you'd never usually go to, and go, for example:
- dog show
- dance championship
- basketball match

Try a sport. Pick a fresh one and spend the next three years mastering it.

2. Go somewhere new.

Take a short break to explore a place you've never been. Act as if you have a friend visiting from out of town and take yourself sightseeing in your home city.

3. Learn something new (whether or not you are good at it).

Be inspired by Peter Drucker who studied and mastered a different skill every three years. Be inspired too by this Zimbabwe proverb:

> If you can walk, you can dance;
> if you can talk, you can sing.

Try music. Did you inherit a musical instrument e.g. violin, clarinet, piano? Do you wish you could play? Don't die with your music still in you. Find a music teacher, perhaps one who specialises in teaching adults to play recognisable tunes by ear for self-entertainment rather than learning to read music and practice for exams. (Adults learning an instrument want a quick win.)

Singing. Whether or not you've been told you sing out of tune, find a singing teacher. Did you know that if you can successfully distinguish difference in pitch — whether two notes are the same or different, higher or lower, going up or going down — you can most likely be taught to sing in tune? To test your pitch, search on the web for 'pitch sensitivity test' or 'test your sense of pitch' to locate an online test which tests your pitch perception. If you are successful on the test, then you might feel comfortable to get lessons; then you can join a choir or acapella group or barbershop quartet or simply sing karaoke. (Singing is good for the brain.)

4. *Write down your goals.*

Dream something new. At start of each year, write a list of new year's resolutions. Start a bucket list, pick one item at a time off the list and make a plan to do it. Make a vision board by pasting cut-out images from magazines or printed off the web onto a large piece of coloured cardboard to form a collage representing your goals, dreams and perfect life; (or create a digital vision board). Categories could be Time, Energy, Wisdom, Money, Love, Creativity, Career, Travel, whatever. You choose. Olympic athletes and sporting teams have successfully used visualisation techniques for decades; it works.

5. *Draw something, make something, repair something.*

Buy some art supplies, go to a park and paint what you see. Locate an art class and enrol (whether or not you are good at art). Learn to sew or knit or weave or do woodwork or sculpt, anything. Just get started.

6. *Write something.*

Each one of us has a story. Express your ideas to the world. You have a contribution to make. Start a memoir. Start a blog. Start that book. Write your book one blog article at a time (like this one). Fall in love with poetry and write a poem. Read Japanese haiku then write your own. Research your local area and write a community history. Study the genealogy of your family and write its history going back generations. Join a writer's group to connect with like-minded people, to receive feedback on your writing and grow as a writer. Groups can provide critique, others are a social opportunity to give one another support, motivation, and ideas.

7. *Bed, Bath and Bus.*

Three likely situations where new ideas spring to mind are bed, bath and bus:

- going to sleep or upon awakening
- in the bath or shower
- while travelling — bus, plane, train, car

Capture ideas as they come up either by carrying a paper notebook and pen, or add notes on your digital device, or email a message to yourself, or create a calendar reminder. Bursts of brilliance are fleeting and soon forgotten if not captured.

8. *Read more.*

Read something different. Successful people read books and read widely. Be well read.

HOW TO BRAINSTORM: ALWAYS LOOK FOR THE SECOND RIGHT ANSWER

When making decisions or solving a problem, instead of leaping onto the first solution that comes to mind, engage in a structured brainstorm to discover a better solution, and here's how to do it.

Brainstorming method can be used for:

- marketing tactics
- innovation
- new product development
- company strategy and decisions
- anything new and better

TIP: Make this a pen and paper exercise. Many of the best authors write their first draft using pen and paper rather than keyboard. The act of writing with pen in hand on paper activates areas of the brain conducive to creative thinking. Choose a space and time where you won't be interrupted.

Method

Step 1. Pose a question

Select a fresh piece of paper or page of a notebook. Write a question top of the page. My wording usually starts with, 'What are 20 possible . . . ', for example:

- What are 20 possible ways to use technology to create a better experience for our customers?
- What are 20 possible low cost, high value items to add to our customer offering?
- What are 20 possible ways to improve how we onboard new team members?
- What are 20 ways our Product/service is different from the competition?
- What are 20 possible ways to provide after-sales customer service so you stay top of mind?
- What are 20 possible ways to stay in touch with a prospect while making the decision to buy?
- *What are 20 possible questions to brainstorm?* (This one question yields a mother-lode of questions to explore!)

Step 2. Write Numbers 1 To 20 Down The Page, Left Hand Side.
Why 20?

Because the first ten ideas are fast, asking for 20 ideas forces your creative brain to kick in. I've often found my best solution was actually idea 19 or 20.

Step 3. List plausible options and don't stop until you have 20.
The first few ideas most likely will arrive easily. But around idea 11 or 12, you may experience a lull in the flow of possible solutions.

That's good! Why?

Psychologists tell us that creativity is often preceded by a mental blank. So hang in there. Staying with the problem until another thought comes to you is part of the process. And then comes the second wind. Wave after wave of new possible solutions. You may even find you go beyond 20 ideas to 22 or 23. (And often it's those last ideas which are the most elegant.)

Step 4. Apply the four principles of brainstorming.

A) Quantity

Go for quantity, 20 or more, and don't stop till you get there.

B) Random Order

Let ideas come in random order (especially if doing a group brainstorm. Don't stop the flow by saying, 'let's look at one area at a time').

C) Suspend Judgement

Don't judge whether an idea is practical, cost-effective, been done before, or any other criteria. At this stage, all ideas are equal. If a thought comes to you, write it down, so your brain can move on to the next random idea.

D) Springboard

If there is a temporary lull in the flow, look back at suggestions already recorded in your list and consider how you can change — extend, reduce, magnify, do the opposite — an idea to propel you to a fresh idea.

Step 5. Select the best solution

Once 20 ideas have been generated, highlight or circle your three favourite options, re-consider those three, decide on first one to action, then action that.

Use this idea-generation method to define best course of action whenever you have a course of action to choose. Often your second 'right' answer is the most elegant.

Trigger Questions

Have on hand a list of trigger questions to refer to, such as:

- What can we **start** doing?
- What can we **stop** doing?
- What can we do **more of**?
- What can we do **less of**?
- What can we **improve**?

Group Brainstorming

Use this idea-generation method with a team for them to co-create a decision, a course of action or continuous improvement.

Instead of pen and paper, use a paper flipchart, poster size paper. Pose a question, write it at the top, pre-draw numbers one to twenty, then add ideas in random order as they are suggested.

Set A Time-Limit

To avoid a time blow-out, do set a time limit. Perhaps start with the whole team, then after a time, say 30 minutes, if 20 ideas have not yet been reached, either reduce group size to the most active participants or adjourn the meeting with an instruction to come back next meeting with fresh suggestions to finish the brainstorm.

Where Does The Word Brainstorming Come From?

Alex Osborn is known as creator of the brainstorming technique. His book, *Applied Imagination* was published in 1953.[14] Brainstorming by itself may not be sufficient. To fine-tune your ideas, you can use other complementary idea-generation techniques. Brainstorming is just one method.

WHERE ARE THE GAPS IN YOUR WORK/LIFE BALANCE?

A life well-lived is a life full of joy and great relationships, a life of success and abundance, a long life of good health and wellbeing.

Here's a short exercise in self-discovery; four quality questions.

Happiness

Happiness includes love and connection, healthy relationships with family and friends, knowing someone loves you, people like you, making time for your children, keeping friends, making new friends.

Quality Question #1

What is one thing you are not doing now, that if you did, would make a positive difference to your level of personal happiness?

Achievement

Achievement includes success, wealth, recognition, growth, learning, qualifications, wisdom.

What have you achieved that you feel proud of? Perhaps not all achievement is money-driven?

Quality Question #2

What is one thing you are not doing now, that if you did, would make a positive difference to your sense of personal achievement?

Contribution

What is your contribution to a better world? Is it:

- making a difference
- donating to your favourite charity, (your money or your time)
- leaving a legacy.

Perhaps it's as simple as growing a garden, planting trees.

Quality Question #3

What is one thing you are not doing now, that if you did, would make a positive contribution to a better world?

Health And Wellbeing

'Why me?' people ask themselves when their doctor tells them bad news. Prevention is better than cure. You are a body, not a ghost-like mind. Your body takes you everywhere. What have you done for it lately that promotes good health and wellbeing?

How do you keep your engine purring? Exercise, playing a sport, dancing, energetic walking?

Are you eating well, staying slim? Getting enough sleep? Regular medical check-ups? Is there a niggling pain you've been ignoring? Have you quit smoking yet? Do you drink enough water?

Loma Linda University Researchers found[15] higher consumption of water helps lower risk of heart disease by up to 60%.

Do you exercise regularly? Here's a tip:

- Schedule exercise as if it's an appointment. Write it in your diary. Instead of performing exercise when you have time — make an appointment, with yourself.

Out of a scale of ten, how you would rate your level of health, energy and vitality?

Quality Question #4

What is one thing you are not doing now, that if you did, would make a positive difference to your health and wellbeing?

Action

Spot places that need more attention and fill in the gaps.

HOW TO BOOST YOUR EMOTIONAL INTELLIGENCE

High emotional intelligence is responsible for productive harmony at work, successful relationships with loved ones and friends, and an inner sense of calm and emotional balance.

For an organisation to evolve from good to great, it requires the people in the business to work well together. Lack of trust, unresolved conflicts or resentment, or individuals not understanding how their actions impact others can be roadblocks to productivity and delivering great results in the workplace.

Unlike IQ (intelligence quotient), there are not as many measurements of emotional quotient or intelligence (EQ or EI).

Academics Salovey and Mayer first coined the term emotional intelligence in 1990.[16] They defined it as ability to:

1. perceive emotions
2. use emotions
3. understand emotions
4. manage emotions.

With publication of Daniel Goleman's bestseller, *Emotional Intelligence*[17] in 1995, the term became popularised.

Research shows

- EQ skills separate high-achievers from average performers
- managers high in EQ outperform their targets by 20%
- salespeople selected on EQ outperform others by 40%
- leaders who display constructive behaviours have high EQ and the business grows.

So what attributes indicate high emotional intelligence?

Self-Awareness

Self-awareness is a quality of EQ; knowing what you are feeling and why you are feeling it.

People Reading

Ability to read the emotions and non-verbal cues of others is also important.

The *Reading the Eyes in the Mind*[18] test assesses how well you can accurately read which emotion an individual is experiencing by what you see in their eyes. The test presents 37 photos of pairs of eyes with a choice of four emotions, e.g. ashamed, nervous, suspicious, indecisive.

Accurately reading emotions of people around you means you are sensitive and responsive to people's feelings. That's EQ.

Stimulus Response

'Between stimulus and response there is a space. In that space is our power to choose our response.' [19]

When a bad experience happens to us, we can either respond with a knee-jerk reaction or pause a moment to stabilise our feelings and consider our best response. An emotionally intelligent person has mastery over their emotions and emotional responses. If you can reflect and consider before reacting, you are demonstrating EQ.

Attitude

Our emotions influence both what we think about and how we think. If you are in a positive mood you will see things differently than when in a negative mood.

Optimism-Pessimism

When something bad happens to an optimist, they view it as temporary and a one-off event. But when a negative experience happens to a pessimist, they regard it as permanent and universal. A pessimist might even respond to such an event with, 'That always happens to me!'

Here's An Optimism/Pessimism Indicator Question.

You gain weight over the holidays and you can't lose it. What is your response, A or B?

> A. Diets don't work.
> B. The diet I tried didn't work.

If you answered B, *The diet I tried didn't work*', you've taken an optimistic approach; failure is temporary. If your response is A, *Diets don't work*', then that's how a pessimist views events; failure is permanent.

Are Optimists Happier In Life?

Pessimists may view the world (according to them) 'realistically'. Optimists may be under an illusion, but it can be argued they experience more joy in the moment. Growing evidence links an optimistic thinking style with lower risk of cancer, heart disease, stroke, respiratory disease and infection.[20]

Stress Tolerance

Ability to tolerate stress and being slow to express frustration indicates high EQ.

Here are some questions to ask yourself:

1. When treated in an unfair manner or not shown due respect or consideration, can I avoid becoming too angry or lashing out?
2. Can I maintain emotional equilibrium and stop myself from getting too down when I experience negative events?
3. Can I prevent myself becoming overly worried about things?
4. When I do get upset, can I calm myself down and bounce back emotionally?

Being resilient means staying emotionally buoyant, bouncing back after an upset and not catastrophising i.e. viewing an inconvenience or disruption as, on the scale of things, worse than it really is.

Resilience

12-step recovery programs use the Serenity Prayer, 'God, grant me the serenity to accept the things I cannot change; Courage to change the things I can, and Wisdom to know the difference.'[21]

It requires emotional intelligence to achieve this clarity.

The Two Marshmallow Test

This is the scenario. You are given a marshmallow, but here's the deal. You can choose to eat it now; or if you can wait 15 minutes, and not eat that marshmallow, you'll be given a second one.

Impulse Control And Delayed Gratification

Research at Stanford University showed the ability to wait for a second marshmallow indicates future success in life and career.[22] Dunedin

University research focused on the relationship between childhood self-control and social measures such as health, wealth and crime.[23]

Could you wait for the second marshmallow?

Flexibility

In summary, an emotionally intelligent person is able to adjust their feelings, thoughts and behaviours to changing situations and conditions. They are open to different ideas and ways of doing things. They are able to look at the brighter side of life and maintain a positive attitude even when times are tough. They are good at problem-solving and able to identify problems as well as generate and implement solutions.

Where To From Here?

You can increase your self-awareness by:

- observing your reactions
- naming your emotions; 'What am I feeling right now?'
- after a negative encounter, stop, reflect what you are feeling and why
- listening to your tone of voice when you are happy, stressed, tired, hungry.

And if you have opportunity to complete a psychometric test or personality profile, they help you reflect on your strengths and weaknesses and aid you to understand yourself, understand others.

REFERENCES

The quotes, anecdotes and ideas described in this book were accumulated from a variety of sources over a number of years. While we've made every attempt to fully attribute the origin of each of these items, the author may have been unable to list some sources in the detail preferred.

1. REINVENT

1. Vilfredo Pareto, Cours d'économie politique professé a l'université de Lausanne. Vol. I 1896; Vol. II, 1897.

2. NPR, Langfitt, Frank, *This American Life*, podcast, NUMMI 2015, Retrieved from https://www.thisamericanlife.org/561/nummi-2015

3. Edmondson, Amy C., (August 26, 2014), *Teaming: How Organizations Learn, Innovate, and Compete in the Knowledge Economy*, Jossey-Bass Pfeiffer, ISBN: 978-0787970932.

4. Thompson, Bob, (September 1, 2013), *Worst to First: How Five Customer-Centric Habits Enabled Sprint's Dramatic Turnaround*, CustomerThink Corp., Retrieved from https://customerthink.com/worst_to_first_how_five_customer_centric _habits_enabled_sprints_turnaround/

2. LEAD FROM THE FRONT

1. Leimbach, Michael, Ph.D, (2006), 'Redefining Employee Satisfaction: Business Performance, Employee Fulfillment, and Leadership Practices' (Research Report), *Wilson Learning*.

2. AON Hewitt, (2013), 2013 Trends in Global Employee Engagement.

3. Handy, Charles, (1995), *The Empty Raincoat*, Random House, London, ISBN: 978-0099301257

4. *Shalom in the Home*, American reality television series, hosted by Rabbi Shmuley Boteach debuted April 10, 2006, on TLC. A second and last season of the series began March 4, 2007.

5. Chartier, Emile, Propos sur le Religion no. 74 (1938), he adopted the pseudonym, Alain, in homage to the 15th-century Norman poet, Alain Chartier.

6. Garvin, David A.; Wagonfeld, Alison Berkley; and Kind, Liz; (April 2013), 'Google's Project Oxygen: Do Managers Matter?', *Harvard Business School,* Case 313-110.

3. ENGAGE

1. Wiley, J. W., (2010), 'The impact of effective leadership on employee engagement'. *Empl. Rel. Today,* 37: 47 — 52. doi:10.1002/ert.20297

2. Oehler, Ken; Stomski, Lorraine; Kustra-Olszewska, Magdalena; (November 7, 2014), 'What Makes Someone an Engaging Leader?', *Harvard Business Review.*

3. Duhigg, Charles, (February, 2016), *What Google Learned From Its Quest to Build the Perfect Team,* The New York Times Magazine, Retrieved from https://www.nytimes.com/2016/02/28/magazine/what-google-learned-from-its-quest-to-build-the-perfect-team.html

4. *Reading The Mind in the Eyes* test, developed by Prof. Simon Baron-Cohen et al. at University of Cambridge. Retrieved from http://socialintelligence.labinthe wild.org

5. Edmondson, Amy C., (June 1999), 'Psychological Safety and Learning Behavior in Work Teams', *Administrative Science Quarterly,* Vol. (2), p. 353.

6. Novak, David C. and Boswell, John, (2007,, The Education of an Accidental CEO: Lessons Learned from the Trailer Park to the Corner Office. Crown Business, New York, ISBN: 978-0307451798.

7. Kotter, John P., (2012), *Leading Change,* Harvard Business Review Press, Revised edition, ISBN: 978-1422186435

8. Lund, Dr. Paddi, (1997), *Building the Happiness Centred Business,* pp. 144-145. Solutions Press, Capalaba, ISBN: 978-0646212746

4. INFLUENCE

1. Ebbinghaus, Hermann,(1885), *Memory: A contribution to experimental psychology.* New York: Dover. Hermann Ebbinghaus, (1850 — 1909) was a German psychologist who pioneered the experimental study of memory and discovered the Serial Position Effect. In remembering lists, he observed that people are more likely to remember items at start and end of lists. These effects are also called Primacy and Recency Effects.

2. Tversky, Amos; and Kahneman, Daniel, (October 1986), 'Rational Choice and the Framing of Decisions', *The Journal of Business*, Vol. *59*(4), Part 2: The Behavioral Foundations of Economic Theory. pp. S251-S278, Stable URL: http://www.jstor.org/stable/2352759

3. Kahneman, Daniel, (2011), *Thinking, Fast and Slow*, Farrar, Straus and Girous, New York, p. 88, 367 ISBN: 978-0374275631.

5. INCREASE PRODUCTIVITY

1. Scott M Cutlip's, (1994), *The Unseen Power: Public Relations: A History* refers to 1918 as the year of Lee and Schwab's meeting. Alec Mackenzie's (1972) *The Time Trap* and Mary Kay's (1995) *You Can Have It All* both reference the story as well.

2. McGhee, Sally, (2005) Take Back Your Life!: Using Microsoft Office Outlook to Get Organized and Stay Organized, Microsoft Press, Washington, USA, p. 56.

3. Parkinson, Cyril Northcote, (November 1955), *Parkinson's Law*, The Economist. 'Work expands so as to fill the time available for its completion'. This since became known as Parkinson's Law. Retrieved from https://www.economist.com/node/14116121

4. DeMers, Jason, (February 9, 2017), *Do You Have 'Shiny Object' Syndrome? What It Is and How to Beat It*, Entreprenuer, Retrieved from https://www.entrepreneur.com/article/288370

6. LOVE YOUR CUSTOMERS

1. Lennon, John and McCartney, Paul, (1969), *The End*, Album: Abbey Road, The Beatles, Apple Records.

2. LeBoeuf, Michael, (2000), *How to Win Customers and Keep Them for Life*, Berkley, New York. For twenty years Michael LeBoeuf was professor of management at University of New Orleans, retiring as Professor Emeritus at age 47 in 1989.

3. Carlzon, Jan, (1987), *Moments of Truth*, Cambridge, MA: Ballinger Publishing.

4. Ebbinghaus, Hermann, (1885), *Memory: A contribution to experimental psychology*. New York: Dover. Hermann Ebbinghaus, (1850 — 1909) was a German psychologist who pioneered the experimental study of memory and discovered the Serial Position Effect. In remembering lists, he observed that people are

more likely to remember items at start and end of lists. These effects are also called Primacy and Recency Effects.

5. Gneezy, A. and Epley, N. (2014), 'Worth keeping but not exceeding asymmetric consequences of breaking versus exceeding promises', *Social Psychological and Personality Science,* Vol. *5*(7), pp. 796-804.

7. COMMUNICATE

1. Levine, Rick; Locke, Christopher; Searls, Doc: and Weinberger, David; (2001), *The Cluetrain Manifesto : The End Of Business As Usual,* Cambridge (Mass.), Basic Books, ASIN: B00MDAMJ18.

2. (1866), *The Companion Letter Writer: A guide to correspondence on all subjects,* Frederick Warne & Co, London/New York. Updated edition: Kessinger Publishing, (2010), ISBN: 978-1165090600.

3. Royal Mail, (2003), 'Typos cost UK business over £700 million a year'. In Ott, Philomena, (2007), *How to Manage Spelling Successfully,* Routledge, p.40, ISBN: 978-0415407328.

4. Penman, John, *Record Business Insider: Business In Brief,* Daily Record, Retrieved from https://www.dailyrecord.co.uk/news/business-consumer/record-business-insider-business-in-brief-930946

5. Boyd, Brian, (November 25, 2005), *Out From Under His Own Shadow,* The Irish Times, Retrieved from https://www.irishtimes.com/culture/out-from-under-his-own-shadow-1.521416

8. PRESENT PERSUASIVELY

1. Foundation for Young Australians, *The New Basics: Big data reveals the skills young people need for the New Work Order,* Retrieved from https://www.fya.org.au/wp-content/uploads/2016/04/The-New-Basics_Update_Web.pdf

2. Gladwell, Malcolm, (2005), *Blink: The Power of Thinking Without Thinking,* Little, Brown and Company, New York, ISBN: 978-0316010665.

3. Van Edwards, Vanessa, (2015), *5 Secrets of a Successful TED Talk,* Huffington Post, Retrieved from https://www.huffingtonpost.com/vanessa-van-edwards/5-secrets-of-a-successful_b_6887472.html

4. Office of the Registrar General & Census Commissioner, India, 2011 Census Data, Retrieved from http://censusindia.gov.in/Census_And_You/age_ structure _and_marital_status.aspx

5. Carter, Judy, (2001), The Comedy Bible: From Stand-up to Sitcom — The Comedy Writer's Ultimate How-To Guide, Fireside, New York. p. 72, ISBN: 0-7432-0125-6.

6. (October 24-25, 1992), 'Kindling the Fire of Curiosity: Professor Julius Sumner Miller on What is Needed to be a Good Teacher', *The Weekend Australian*, p. 30, Retrieved from http://www.wilderdom.com/quotes/educa tion/JuliusSumnerMillerOnEducation.html

7. Rudyard Kipling's (1865-1936) poem, first published 1900, part of the collection, *Just So Stories*, published 1902.

9. SKYROCKET YOUR SALES

1. Jung, Carl Gustav, (1966), *The Practice of Psychotherapy: Essays on the Psychology of the Transference and other Subjects* (Collected Works Vol. *16*). Princeton, New Jersey, Princeton University Press, ISBN: 978-0691018706.

2. Baker, Michael, (February 2014), *What Is The Best Time For Cold Calls?*, RAMP — the InsightSquared Blog, Retrieved from http://www.insightsquared.com/ 2014/02/what-is-the-best-time-for-cold-calls/

3. Freese, Thomas, (2013), Secrets of Question-Based Selling: How the Most Powerful Tool in Business Can Double Your Sales Results, Sourcebooks, Second edition, p. 80, ISBN: 978-1402287527

4. Rackham, Neil, (1994) *Spin Selling*, McGraw Hill, New York, ASIN: B0081USDU0.

5. Ziglar, Zig, (2004) *Secrets Of Closing A Sale*, Revell (updated edition), ISBN: 978-0800759759.

6. Cialdini, Robert B. Ph.D., (2006), *Influence: The Psychology of Persuasion*, Harper Paperbacks, New York; Revised edition, ISBN: 978-0061241895.

10. SHARPEN YOUR OFFICE ETTIQUETTE

1. Gladwell, Malcolm, (2005), *Blink: The Power of Thinking Without Thinking*, Little, Brown and Company, New York, ISBN: 978-0316010665.

2. http://www.galaxyresearch.com.au/

3. Millar Chris, and Mendick, Robert, (21 June 2005), 'Ketchupgate' Lawyer Quits Firm, *Evening Standard*, Retrieved from https://www.standard.co.uk/news/ketchupgate-lawyer-quits-firm-7169537.html

4. Royal Mail, (2003), 'Typos cost UK business over £700 million a year'. In Ott, Philomena, (2007), *How to Manage Spelling Successfully*, Routledge, p.40, ISBN: 978-0415407328.

5. AAP, (October 27, 2004), *Latham In A Flap Over Howard Handshake*, Sydney Morning Herald, Retrieved from https://www.smh.com.au/articles/2004/10/27/1098667806417.html

6. (2003), 'Lenox Gift-Giving and Etiquette Survey', Lenox, Retrieved from https://www.businesswire.com/news/home/20031022005118/en/Annual-Lenox-Survey-34-Rank-Peoples-Manners

11. GATHER WISDOM

1. Survey conducted March 7 – April 4, (2016), *Book Reading 2016*, Pew Research Centre, 2016, Retrieved from http://www.pewinternet.org

2. Abadzi, Helen, (2003), *Improving adult literacy outcomes: lessons from cognitive research for developing countries*, Directions in Development, Washington, D.C.: The World Bank, P.18. Retrieved from http://documents.worldbank.org/curated/en/488381468739264375/Improving-adult-literacy-outcomes-lessons-from-cognitive-research-for-developing-countries

3. Orwell, George, (1946), *Animal Farm*, Signet, ASIN: B0018XFL0C.

4. Manguel, Alberto, (1996), *The History of Reading*, HarperCollins, London, p. 41, ISBN: 0 00 255006 7

5. Saint Augustine. Confessions, VI, 3, in *The History of Reading*, Alberto Manguel, (1996), HarperCollins, London, p. 42, ISBN: 0 00 255006 7

6. Saenger, Paul, (1997), *Space Between Words: The Origins of Silent Reading*, Stanford University Press, p. 6, ISBN: 978-0804726535

7. Sean Shannon, record-holder, fastest talker, 655 words per minute, 1995, *The Guinness Book of Records*, Guinness World Records Limited, ISBN: 978-1910561720.

8. Morrison, Robert (First published 1828, Reproduction 2012), *Vocabulary Of The Canton Dialect: Chinese Words And Phrases*, Nabu Press, ISBN: 978-1286588352.

9. Sunday, Nina, (2004), *Speed Reading: Read Faster, Smarter and Easier*, online program, Retrieved from https://www.udemy.com/speed-reading-read-faster-smarter-and-easier/

10. Macroreading® is scanning around twice-as-fast as comfortable to gain working knowledge of a document.

11. Sunday, Nina, (2011), *Brainpower Smart Study: How To Study Effectively Using a Tested and Proven 8-step Study Method*, Brainpower Training, Sydney, pp. 9-11, ISBN: 978 0 9751941 5 7.

12. Ward, Marguerite (16 November 2016), 'Warren Buffett's Reading Routine Could Make You Smarter, Science Suggests', Retrieved from https://www.cnbc.com/2016/11/16/ warren- buffetts-reading-routine-could-make-you-smarter-suggests-science.html

13. Siebold, Steve, (2010), *How Rich People Think*, London House, London, ISBN: 978-0-9755003-4-7.

14. Strauss, Neil, (November 15, 2017), *Elon Musk: The Architect of Tomorrow*, Rolling Stone, Retrieved from https://www.rollingstone.com/culture/features/elon-musk-inventors-plans-for-outer-space-cars-finding-love-w511747

15. Youshaei, Jon, (March 6, 2018), 'Elon Musk's 10 Secrets To Success', Forbes, Retrieved from https://www.forbes.com/sites/jonyoushaei/2018/03/06/elon-musks-10-secrets-to-success/#2546f6e5281e

16. Elliott, Hannah, (April, 2012), 'The (Formerly) Fast Times of the (Soon-to-Be) Bachelor (Multi) Billionaire', *ForbesLife*, Retrieved from https://www.forbes.com/forbes-life-magazine/2012/0409/feature-elon-musk-paypal-spacex-tesla-fast-times-bachelor-billionaire.html

17. Baer, Drake, (January 8, 2016), *Bill Gates Says Reading 50 Books A Year Gives Him A Huge Advantage*, Tech Insider, Retrieved from http://www.business insider.com/why-bill-gates-reads-50-books-a-year-2015-11?IR=T

18. Retrieved from http://www.anitaroddick.com/aboutanita.php

19. Sunday, Nina, (2004), *Speed Reading: Read Faster, Smarter and Easier*, online program, Retrieved from https://www.udemy.com/speed-reading-read-faster-smarter-and-easier/

12. STAY CURIOUS

1. Elizabeth Gilbert is the #1 New York Times bestselling author of *Eat, Pray, Love*, (2007) as well as *Committed (2011)*, 'What to Do if You *Can't* Find Your Passion', Retrieved from http://www.oprah.com/spirit/elizabeth-gilbert-on-the-importance-of-curiosity

2. Falk, Dean; Lepore, Frederick E.; Noe, Adrianne, (1 April 2013), 'The cerebral cortex of Albert Einstein: a description and preliminary analysis of unpublished photographs'; *Brain*, Vol. *136*(4), pp. 1304 — 1327, doi.org/10.1093/brain/aws295

3. Nottebohm Fernando; Nottebohm Marta E.; and Crane Linda, (1986), 'Developmental and seasonal changes in canary song and their relation to changes in the anatomy of song-control nuclei', *Behavioral and Neural Biology*, Vol. *46*(3) pp. 445 — 71.

4. Eriksson, Peter S.; Perfilieva, Ekaterina; Björk-Eriksson, Thomas; Alborn, Ann-Marie; Nordborg Claes; Peterson Daniel A.; & Gage, Fred H., (November 1998), 'Neurogenesis In The Adult Human Hippocampus', *Nature Medicine*, Vol 4, pp. 1313 — 1317, doi:10.1038/3305

5. Maguire, Eleanor A.; Gadian, David G.; Johnsrude, Ingrid S.; Good, Catriona D.; Ashburner, John; Frackowiak, Richard S. J.; Frith, Christopher D., (April 11, 2000), 'Navigation-related structural change in the hippocampi of taxi drivers'. *PNAS (Proceedings of the National Academy of Sciences)*, Vol. *97*(8), pp. 4398 — 4403. doi:10.1073/pnas.070039597

6. Draganski, Bogdan; Gaser, Christian; Busch, Volker; Schuierer, Gerhard; Bogdahn, Ulrich; & May, Arne, (22 January, 2004), 'Neuroplasticity: changes in grey matter induced by training', *Nature*, Vol. *427*, pp. 311-312, doi:10.1038/427311a

7. Drucker, Peter F; and Nakauchi, Isao, (1997), Drucker on Asia: A dialogue between Peter Drucker and Isao Nakauchi, Routledge, p. 105, ISBN: 978-0750631327.

8. Prepared text of the Commencement address delivered by Steve Jobs, CEO of Apple Computer and of Pixar Animation Studios, (June 12, 2005), Retrieved from https://news.stanford.edu/2005/06/14/jobs-061505/

9. Clark, Dorie, (2016), Stand Out: How to Find Your Breakthrough Idea and Build a Following Around It, Portfolio, ISBN: 978-0241247013.

10. Fuller, Richard Buckminster (2002), *Critical Path,* Macmillan, p. 38. ISBN: 0312174918. Buckminster Fuller (1895 — 1983) was an American architect, inventor, philosopher and systems theorist who invented the geodesic dome and created the terms 'Spaceship Earth', 'synergetics' and 'ephemeralization'.

11. Gardner, Howard, (1983), *Frames of Mind: The Theory of Multiple Intelligences,* Basic Books, ISBN 0133306143

12. ten Brinke, Lisanne F; Bolandzadeh, Niousha; Nagamatsu Lindsay S.; et al,(April 7, 2014), 'Aerobic exercise increases hippocampal volume in older women with probable mild cognitive impairment: a 6-month randomised controlled trial', *British Journal of Sports Medicine,* Vol.*49*(4), pp. 248-254, dx.doi.org/10.1136/bjsports-2013-093184

13. Hillman, Charles H; Pontifex, MB; Raine, LB; Castelli, DM; Hall, EE; Kramer, AF; (March 31, 2009), 'The effect of acute treadmill walking on cognitive control and academic achievement in preadolescent children', *Neuroscience;* Vol. *159*(3), pp. 1044-54. doi: 10.1016/j.neuroscience.2009.01.057

14. Osborn, Alex F., (1979), *Applied Imagination,* Scribner, New York, ASIN: B000Y0A95C.

15. Chan, J., et al, (2002), 'Water, Other Fluids, and Fatal Coronary Heart Disease', *American Journal of Epidemiology,* Vol. *155*(9) pp. 827-833, doi.org/10.1093/aje/155.9.827

16. Salovey, Peter and Mayer, John D., (March 1990), 'Emotional Intelligence', in *Information, Cognition and Personality,* Vol. *9*(3).

17. Goleman, Daniel, (1995), *Emotional Intelligence: Why It Can Matter More Than IQ,* Bantam Books, ISBN: 978-0553095036.

18. *Reading The Mind in the Eyes* test, developed by Prof. Simon Baron-Cohen et al. at University of Cambridge. Retrieved from http://socialintelligence.labinthe wild.org

19. Anonymous. Often credited to Viktor E. Frankl, but this quote does not appear in Frankl's book, *Man's Search For Meaning*. These words were popularized by author Stephen R. Covey in *7 Habits of Highly Effective People*, however, Covey claims he read these words in a book in a library in Hawaii. That library no longer exists. Retrieved from https://quoteinvestigator.com/2018/02/18/response/

20. Kim, Eric S.; Hagan, Kaitlin A.; Grodstein, Francine; DeMeo, Dawn L.; De Vivo, Immaculata; Kubzansky, Laura D.; (January 2017), 'Optimism and Cause-Specific Mortality: A Prospective Cohort Study', *American Journal of Epidemiology*, Vol. 185, pp. 21 – 29.

21. Niebuhr, Ronald, (1892 – 1971), American Theologian, first wrote the Serenity Prayer for a church sermon in Massachusetts as early as 1934.

22. Mischel, Walter; Ebbesen, Ebbe B; October (1970), 'Attention in delay of gratification', *Journal of Personality and Social Psychology*. 16 (2), pp. 329 — 337.

23. Poulton, Richie; Moffitt, Terrie E.; Silva, Phil A., (2015), 'The Dunedin Multidisciplinary Health and Development Study: overview of the first 40 years, with an eye to the future', Social Psychiatry and Psychiatric Epidemiology. 50 (5): 679 — 693. doi:10.1007/s00127-015-1048-8. ISSN 0933-7954

ACKNOWLEDGEMENTS

Thanks and appreciation to everyone who contributed their talents to this project in one way or another. Russell Perks, Helena Bond, Elizabeth Beeton, Mandy McLean, Libby McArdle, Imogen McDonald, Tim Vetter, Lily Sumner, Pip Savaris, Paula Smith.

DISCLAIMER

The material included in this book is designed to provide information and practical tips for readers and give general guidance only. Advice in this book was derived from the author's research and professional experience. No warranties or guarantees are expressed or implied by the content in this book.

Material is compressed and simplified for educational purposes and should not create expectations about how you may deal with any specific matter in particular circumstances. The reader is responsible for their own choices, actions and results.

The publisher accepts no liability for loss or damage that may be suffered by any person or entity that relies on information in this book. The purpose of this book is to increase understanding and awareness of the topic. The material should be used fairly and accurately.

Resources

I trust you enjoyed this book and gained value from some of the ideas. Readers of *Workplace Wisdom for 9 to Thrive* will find additional articles and resources at:

> www.brainpowertraining.com.au/workplacewisdom

To receive a regular burst of inspiration in similar style to the chapters in this book, sign up to receive my blog by email.
Go to:

> www.brainpowertraining.com.au/contact

Nina Sunday

ABOUT THE AUTHOR

Nina Sunday is an international speaker, educator and author. Professional Speakers Australia awarded her CSP designation (Certified Speaking Professional), held by only 12% of professional speakers worldwide.

After working in education, the performing arts, sales and television, Nina founded Australian training company, Brainpower Training, and over two decades grew a network of Facilitators delivering business skills to Top 500 companies, SMEs (small-medium enterprises) and government.

After a decade niching in Speed Reading and Memory, she spent the next 17 years developing and delivering programs in Productivity, Communication, Presentation Skills, Emotional Intelligence, Leadership, Change and Sales. Nina Sunday is the Workplace Maven, empowering managers and teams sharpen their workplace know-how for different thinking, better results.

Qualifications include a Bachelor of Arts and Diploma in Education, plus graduating in Direction and Production Management from the three-year program of the Australian Film, TV and Radio School.

After more than three decades based in Sydney, Nina recently relocated to discover a new-found love of her hometown of Brisbane in Queensland, Australia.